Guaranteed Victory

GUARANTEED
VICTORY

DISCOVERING
THE HIDDEN
TRUTHS
OF
GIDEON'S 300

GUARANTEED
VICTORY

DISCOVERING
THE HIDDEN
TRUTHS
OF
GIDEON'S 300

MATTHEW HESTER

Published by Dominion Publishing
1106 South Highway 14
Greer, SC 29650
DominionChurch.net
Phone 1 (864) 968.5100
Questions/Comments - **info@hesterministries.org**
Printed in the United States of America

For other great resources please visit:
www.HesterMinistries.org

Dedication

This volume is dedicated to the unlikely heroes.
God is calling you out of hiding and breathing new life into your
purpose. Look around, you are in the midst of well doing.
Don't get weary.

Thank you to all who helped to make this book a reality!

Special Thanks - Making It Personal

John & Trishana Bolden - Flora Edwards - Ann Fyall
Van & Verella Golson - Jerry & Martha Hester
Carmen Jefferson - Ellen Lewis - Dave & Nettie Musselman
Brittaney Pearson - Christopher & Victoria Rushing
The Rumer Family (Dana, Easterlan, Zae, Seth and Keturah)
Franklin Waters
The Shaffer Family (Sid, Emily, Maxine and Madeline)

Very Special Thanks - Angel Supporter

Richie & Jan Williams

Special thanks to Chad McMillan and Nettie Musselman
for helping to make this book the best yet!

RECOMMENDATIONS

I want to recommend Guaranteed Victory by Matthew Hester to you, not only to read, but to share with other believers who are hungry to leave the fear based atmospheres of religion to soar into the relationship driven realm of Guaranteed Victory. Matthew Hester draws from his rich heritage as a believer, and even deeper well of being a worshipper to unlock revelation and insight to conquering fear and soaring into victory. I commend him for this book and recommend it to you. Enjoy and share as you move to Guaranteed Victory.

Bishop David Huskins

Author & Presiding Bishop of
The International Communion of Charismatic Churches

On the horizon of Christianity today, there is a fresh and new revolution that is dawning. This revolution is not one of swords and weapons, rather it is a revolution of the pen and tongue. A fresh perspective is dawning that will lay aside the grave clothes of the past moves of God that has laid dormant and unsuccessful to reform the Church and transform nations. What is on the horizon is a "New Covenant Revolution". Apostle Matthew Hester is one of the generals that God has brought through the ranks to help lead His Church into this new day that is dawning.

Matthew successfully relates to his audience by way of revelation that, through proper identification in who we are in Christ Jesus, we have already received all authority to overcome anything and everything that is counterproductive to the will of God for our lives. Through the narrative of Gideon and his company we will recognize who we are, how to overcome fear, and how to ultimately find victory to succeed and live out our life purpose with authority and great expectations!

Matthew successfully moves his readers away from "Old Covenant" thinking and with broad strokes and fine details, paints us the picture of the Finished Work of the Cross, and brings us into a fresh and timely revelation of New Covenant living. Matthew consistently dismantles the smoke and mirrors of today's "religious Christianity" as he eloquently points us away from Law centeredness back to a Christocentric view of scripture. This view in my opinion will be the only way to successfully transform nations and fill all things with the Glory of God.

I encourage you to carefully read each page and meditate on what Matthew has diligently and faithfully written for the Church as was given to Him by the Lord. This is not just another book, this is the beginnings of a Revolution, and you and I have the honor to see the beginnings of this Revolution and Reformation movement that will ultimately change the world for the Glory of God.

Prophet Shane Mason

Author & Lead Pastor of *The King's Church Jacksonville*

In the reading of Guaranteed Victory, there was a revelation that grabbed hold of my spirit: fear is a choice. In this thought, Matthew Hester reveals a truth; people don't see a reason to fight, they only see the thing that causes fear. He explains that when you lack identity, you lack power and spiritual authority and you'll end up being the one hiding in your tent instead of facing your giants. When you understand God has a cause for your life, it will empower you. Matthew shows how this power will cause your giants to fall and release to you the victory He has guaranteed. This book is a must read. It will encourage and strengthen you.

Prophet Rob Sanchez

Author & Founder of *Prophetic First Fruits International Ministries*

An easy read of revelatory truth, that if grasped and understood, will revolutionize your personal life and that of the church as we know it.

In the evolutionary processes of rediscovering the Kingdom Message and authentic Apostolic Christianity, Matthew Hester's book is the very pivot upon which the pendulum swings. He clearly reveals present-day truths to bring the church to its victorious eschatology, helping the readers to understand that this is a journey we are all on, desiring to achieve and reach our destiny, the destiny of Victory established in and through Christ for us.

Matthew does a great job in helping us understand the desperate need for relational identity: that it comes to us, not because of our works, but because of His great work. A crucial point for every believer is to come to understand placement; the joining and the jointing of the Lord. Identity is crucial to destiny, awakening and adjusting our mind sets to be able to belong in meaningful and authoritative relationships. The victory that is ours comes across clearly as Matthew explains and breaks down for us how we are able to identify with the 300 of Gideon.

I look forward to the sequel to this book. There needs to be one.

Apostle Dave Viljoen

Author & Founder of *AWC - Apostolic Working Company*

FOREWORD

The principles and keys that are laid out in Matthew Hester's new book are truly gems. Here is one example: "The massive church in America should have no problem dealing with the issues we currently face, right? If not, maybe we need to examine the church a little deeper. Maybe what we have settled for as the church presently, isn't what God has intended for us to be. Maybe we have bought into the thought that numbers somehow count for strength. In the Kingdom of God, people are weighed, they are not counted."

His lucid assessment of the current state of the church is not an indictment, but rather a diagnosis. The main target in Hester's aim is the fear mindset that most of the church has been influenced by. "The religious church has created a climate of fear by keeping the saints of God in an Old Covenant mindset. This mindset extends towards God, one another, and infiltrates the values we develop throughout the course of our lives. This type of lifestyle produces a judgmental God Who is ready, at a moments notice, to punish us for our failures and mistakes. It causes us to indulge in self condemnation and empowers the cycles of sin and failure that we try so desperately to escape from. If God were truly angry with us, then we would have sufficient reason to be afraid. The truth is that God is not angry with us, and we find abundant proof of this truth in the life and ministry of Jesus."

Matthew Hester doesn't chide his readers; rather he points to the answer, which is to know one's identity firm in Christ: to be unswayable, to become rooted and grounded in love rather than fear. These are not lofty unrelateable concepts meant only for the few. Identity is a universal problem that we all must struggle through at some point in our life. Matthew's approach is grounded in reality and straight to the point. A final quote that I loved from this book was about Gideon's secret... "The great secret of Gideon, is that there is no secret. He was a man that was full of doubt and fear, just like most of us. He struggled with his identity, and he certainly never had himself pegged as a national war hero. At face value, he was an abject failure when it came to building an army. Less than one percent of his group remained, once the fearful and the foolish were sifted. By today's standards, Gideon would be laughed out of the who's who of the church club, and would probably never be heard from again. Fortunately, the Lord is still searching for men and women like Gideon. He is looking for those, who despite their fear and insecurities, are willing to take a step of faith in the face of ridiculous odds."

Dr. Jonathan Welton

Bestselling Author & President of Welton Academy

Contents

Introduction		16
Chapter One	Vital Powers and Strength	20
Chapter Two	Fear Is A Choice	31
Chapter Three	The Spirit Of Fear	37
Chapter Four	Flowing In Power	43
Chapter Five	The High Mountains	53
Chapter Six	Warriors Of Worship	59
Chapter Seven	The Weapons Of War	65
Chapter Eight	The Art Of Unity	73
Chapter Nine	Come Out Of Hiding	79
Chapter Ten	Living In Guaranteed Victory	85
Chapter Eleven	The Peace That Follows	91
Bonus	Have You Considered This	99

GUARANTEED
VICTORY

INTRODUCTION

I have been around ministry for most of my life, and in full time ministry for nearly 15 years. It is interesting the themes that emerge consistently within the local church. I have seen themes of faith, joy, and trust, but I have also seen themes of fear, doubt, and discouragement. Faith, joy, and trust should absolutely be part of the life of the believer, but fear, doubt, and discouragement shouldn't. God has given us power and authority to rule and reign over anything that goes against His nature in us.

I began to seek the Lord on these issues, and it was during this time that I kept going into the famous encounter of Gideon that we find in Judges 6. The more I prayed and researched this amazing showdown between 300 unlikely warriors and an innumerable army of Midianites, I began to see keys emerge to help us overcome the primary factors that produce fear in our lives. I discovered keys that helped to overcome fear, insurmountable odds, issues with authority, trusting God, and more! This is the purpose of this book. I hope to help us gain understanding in key areas that will propel us into greater identity, authority, and victory.

There are three primary points I hope to address and help us all to gain greater understanding concerning. These points are:

A) Fear comes out of misplaced identity.

> *Romans 8:15-*
> *For you did not receive the spirit of slavery to fall back into fear, but you have received the Spirit of adoption as sons, by whom we cry, "Abba! Father!" (ESV)*

The greatest identity that any of us can receive is from our heavenly Father. One of the primary focuses of God in our lives, is to affirm our identity as sons and daughters. Once we truly believe that we are the family of God, we begin to have a tremendous confidence that grows inside. Sons and daughters do not walk around trying to be sons and daughters! They simply ARE what they have come FROM. When you met Jesus as the Lord of your life, all that you were was totally and radically transformed (2 Cor. 5:17)! You are now OF CHRIST and are therefore part of the holy nation (family) of God. Understanding that God is your Father, causes fear to fade away into nothing.

B) Fear comes from not understanding that you're empowered.

> *2 Timothy 1:7-*
> *For God hath not given us the spirit of fear; but of power, and of love, and of a sound mind. (KJV)*

The sons and daughters of God are greatly empowered. In fact, Jesus delegated all power to us that was given to Him (Matt. 28:18-20). If you have been given ALL power, how much power does that leave for anyone or anything that would rise up against you? In the Kingdom of God, power is always directly connected to identity. Thankfully, we not only have the authority of Jesus on us, but His Spirit reigns within us! What could we overcome if we truly believed and flowed in the power God has given us?

C) Fear comes when you have forgotten the cause.

I Samuel 17:29-
And David said, What have I now done? Is there not a cause?
(KJV)

God is not simply for us, but He has also swept us up into the momentum of His goodness from the beginning of time. We are the heirs of the greatest covenant ever established, and have the privilege and grace that comes with it (Rom. 8:17)! When we face difficult and hard times, we need to remind ourselves of the great cause that is within our midst. When we have personal failings and shortcomings, we need to remember who we are in God and how precious we truly are to Him. Our lives are an important ingredient in the plan and purpose of God, and our savor is the strongest it has ever been.

> God is not simply for us, but He has also swept us up into the momentum of His goodness from the beginning of time.

Those who are of the quality of Gideon's 300 know how to resist the propensity to give in to fear. I am not saying that fear is always easy to dismantle, but I am saying that it gets easier to overcome. Fear most often is not defeated with one singular stand in one given moment, but it is an attitude developed over one's life that endures through many situations and circumstances. We must believe that whatever God has called us to be and to do, does not mix well with fear. The church that God is building is free of an identity crisis! The church God is building understands that it is empowered! The church God is building remembers the cause!

As you read this book, allow the Lord to minister to your identity. You are His righteousness. From this perspective, you will see every other area of your life come alive. Come up into the mountains my friends and let's see what God sees as we walk in the *Guaranteed Victory* that He has ordained for us all!

GUARANTEED

VICTORY

CHAPTER ONE
VITAL POWERS AND STRENGTH

Gideon - The Mighty Warrior

> *Judges 6:11-*
> *And there came an angel of the Lord, and sat under an oak*
> *which was in Ophrah, that pertained unto Joash the*
> *Abiezrite: and his son Gideon threshed wheat by the*
> *winepress, to hide it from the Midianites. (KJV)*

When we first meet Gideon, we find him hiding out in fear. He is threshing wheat in a non-typical place because he didn't want the Midianites to find him. When we first encounter Gideon, his identity seems like anything other than that of a mighty warrior. We don't know much about his family other than that his father was an Abiezrite, who was of the tribe of Manasseh. We know that his father had an altar built for Baal at home, and that the first assignment given to Gideon by the Lord was to destroy said altar. When we see the initial snapshot of Gideon's life we can quickly surmise that his identity was not very solid.

Gideon follows the demands of the Lord to overturn the altar of Baal, cut down the grove beside the altar, and build a new one in order to make a sacrifice to the Lord. Gideon did all of the things the Lord asked of him, but he still did them while he was afraid. The next morning the scene was not pleasant, and the people discovered quickly that Gideon was at fault. The crowd demanded Gideon's life, but thankfully his father intervened. The thought Joash posed before the people was fascinating. He made the case that if Baal was a god, then he should plead for himself. Of course, Baal gave no answer and Gideon walked away from the encounter unscathed.

This act brought about a great gathering of the armies of the Midiantes, Amalekites, and the children of the east. We see later in the account just how vast this assembly was. Needless to say, seeing so many enemies gathered together in one place would be very intimidating and discouraging. Fear and doubt were rampant throughout the tribes of Israel. God would have to use someone who was fearless to lead his men into such an overwhelmingly uneven battle. God already had his champion selected. God had already chosen Gideon.

> *Judges 6:34-*
> *But the Spirit of the Lord came upon Gideon, and he blew a*
> *trumpet… (KJV)*

The word for "spirit" used in Judges 6:34 is *ruah* which means "vital powers or strength." I believe that, when Gideon saw he was being backed up by the God of Israel, something shifted radically in his identity. The scared man we met just a day earlier, has now had the vital powers and strength of God come upon him! Experiencing the strength and depth of our God given identity helps us to realize how greatly empowered we are to accomplish outstanding things.

Experiencing the strength and depth of our God given identity helps us to realize how greatly empowered we are to accomplish outstanding things.

What Is Our Identity?

The need for proper understanding of identity is the greatest it has ever been in history! Many believers today have no real understanding of who they are in God, and therefore have no understanding of their authority or assignment. Those that do pursue their identity in God, often approach the topic with a "works based" mentality which, ultimately, cannot help. Our identity as the sons and daughters of God is beautiful and powerful. Developing a picture of what your identity in God truly is, is sublime. Discovering that your identity in God is a gift, is glorious!

> *2 Corinthians 5:17-*
> *Therefore, if anyone is in Christ, the new creation has come: The old has gone, the new is here! (NIV)*

God does not build relationship with us based on our merit. He doesn't look at us and consider what we have or haven't done. God sees us and approves and validates us through Jesus! God doesn't think in terms of what you do and don't deserve. He sees Jesus, (you are all wrapped up in Him) and Jesus deserves all blessing, favor, joy, and victory! The relationship God has with us, is based on what Jesus has accomplished concerning us, and not what we have accomplished ourselves. The righteousness of Jesus is our righteousness and it is the "GIFT OF GOD!"

> *Romans 5:17-*
> *For if, by the trespass of the one man, death reigned through that one man, how much more will those who receive God's abundant provision of grace and of the gift of righteousness reign in life through the one man, Jesus Christ! (NIV)*

Today, when God looks at you, He sees Jesus! He looks at you, and His thoughts are to bless you, prosper you, and release His favor on you without measure. God desires to release love on you that you cannot earn. The truth is, we couldn't pay the price demanded for our sins even if we gave our lives for them. Jesus initiated a New Covenant for us, and now causes us to be seated with Him on His throne of righteousness, and to rule and reign with Him in life and grace.

When God sees us, He also sees His perfect Son. He is well pleased with us! This is not dependent on what we do right or wrong. We do not fall out of His grace because we make mistakes or misbehave. The perfect sacrifice of Jesus is not afraid of our failure, neither are its blessings removed when we mess up. Stop believing the lie that your mistakes have more power than the blood of Jesus! Believe in the work accomplished by Jesus on the cross!

John 3:14-15-
And as Moses lifted up the serpent in the wilderness, even so
must the Son of man be lifted up: That whosoever believeth in
him should not perish, but have eternal life. (KJV)

How does one receive eternal life? Do we receive life by perfect obedience, never making another mistake, keeping all of Gods commandments, praying enough, and fasting enough? No! We are simply instructed to believe! Believe in what? We must believe in what Jesus accomplished on the cross! He took all of our sins and gave us all of His righteousness! He took our worst (past, present, and future) and gave to us His righteousness and eternal life. Believe in what He has accomplished for us!

> He took our worst (past, present, and future) and gave to us
> His righteousness and eternal life.

John 15:4-5-
Abide in me, and I in you. As the branch cannot bear fruit of
itself, except it abide in the vine; no more can ye, except ye abide
in me. I am the vine, ye are the branches: He that abideth in me,
and I in him, the same bringeth forth much fruit: for without me
ye can do nothing. (KJV)

Without Jesus we can do nothing. This is a picture of what it is to abide in the grace (the undeserved, unmerited, and unearned favor) of the Lord in our lives. It is also imperative for us to remember the dynamic shift in our identity once we come to the saving knowledge of Jesus. We become branches of the vine! Before you were a branch, you were a sinner. Once you became a branch, you were no longer a sinner. Your identity was completely and totally destroyed and rebuilt by the hands of the King. You are now a new creation!

In the times when we fail today, we are still the righteousness of God. How? Our righteousness comes from Jesus and not of our own accomplishments and despite our mistakes. In the same way that a butterfly can never imagine becoming a caterpillar again, one who is made the righteousness of God in Christ, cannot imagine being a sinner again! Once you have a sure foundation in the righteousness of Jesus, you have no desire to go back. This understanding of identity is what gives us the power to overcome any and all sins and failures.

I like to draw the connection between identity, and the truth we discovered in Judges 6 earlier in this chapter. When we begin to understand who we are in God and Who God is in us, we have His divine Spirit (ruah) come upon us. In other words, proper identity for the believer is likened to receiving the vital powers and strength of God, in order that we might be of greater usefulness in the hands of the King! You are the righteousness of God. The gift has been given and all you have to do is believe and receive.

GUARANTEED
VICTORY

CHAPTER TWO
FEAR IS A CHOICE

The Bible is full of spiritual truth. In fact, most churches that are gathering today all over the world, will most likely examine a portion of Scripture that the pastor will break down to a certain level, so that the truth can be applied to everyone who hears it. I love the spiritual principles we gain from Scripture and I preach them myself, but there is more to the Word of God than just spiritual principles. If we are not careful, the bulk of our Christian experience will be collecting spiritual principles to impact and enrich our lives only on spiritual levels.

We have to remember that the events that played out in Scripture dealt with real people in real situations. Yes, there are great spiritual principles to learn from Moses, but he actually led his people free from captivity. You can learn principles of courage from the life of David, but he actually killed Goliath, and David actually became king. I fear that much of how we relate to Scripture has created a disconnect for how we should use it to impact our culture and society in a real way.

Making A Real Impact

The professing church globally, is massive in its scale. The most recent statistics put people who profess Christian faith to make up just over 32% of the world's population. Let's take people at face value for a moment and assume these numbers are true. If they are, Christianity should be the dominating force throughout the world. Nations such as America, Brazil, Mexico and Great Britain should be beacons of hope for the world to imitate and admire. America, which boasts an 80% profession of Christian faith by its citizens, should be the model of how to run a nation based on Christian principles and values. Sadly, we are presently witnessing the opposite of what statistics should dictate.

Could it be that we are witnessing some of the symptoms of how many professing believers view the principles of Scripture? Maybe we are so focused on getting spiritual results from the Word of God, that we have forgotten that His Word is also able to bring about actual, physical results. I appreciate having personal peace, but I would love for that peace to permeate my community. I appreciate the love of God, but I want to share that love with everyone I encounter in a real way. God fashioned us in such a way that we are spiritual beings who are capable of making great natural impact.

> God fashioned us in such a way that we are spiritual beings who are capable of making great natural impact.

In America, it seems that our Christian principles are under daily assault. Progressive and humanistic ideas are crammed down our throats and the freedoms we once had without question, are increasingly being put down. The massive church in America should have no problem dealing with the issues we currently face, right? If not, maybe we need to examine the church a little deeper. Maybe what we have settled for as the church presently, isn't what God has intended for us to be. Maybe we have bought into the thought that numbers somehow count for strength. In the Kingdom of God, people   are   weighed,   they   are   not   counted.

When we start counting the company in our midst, it usually doesn't turn out very well. In 1 Chronicles 21, we see King David give in to the desire to count the people of his Kingdom. This is not something God approved of. In the end, God gave David three consequences to choose from and none of them were pleasant. David had to choose between disease, defeat by his enemies, or being dealt with by the hand of God. God showed us this principle multiple times in the Old Testament. We should be more concerned with what God is doing in our midst than we are concerned about how many of us there are.

In the Kingdom of God people are weighed, they are not counted.

The First Separation

> *Judges 7:2-3-*
> *And the LORD said unto Gideon, The people that are with thee are too many for me to give the Midianites into their hands, lest Israel vaunt themselves against me, saying, Mine own hand hath saved me. Now therefore go to, proclaim in the ears of the people, saying, Whosoever is fearful and afraid, let him return and depart early from mount Gilead. And there returned of the people twenty and two thousand; and there remained ten thousand. (KJV)*

When Gideon had gathered together a multitude to face the Midianites, he understood quickly that the odds were not in his favor. No one knows the exact number of the Midiantites that gathered, but there are estimates as high as several hundred thousand. Let's say that the Midiantes gathered exactly 200,000 men. If this was the case, Gideon's initial gathering of 32,000 would have been outmatched 6 to 1. I wonder what Gideon thought. Perhaps he thought, "God is with us. Maybe some of these guys can really fight! Maybe if we catch them by surprise we can pull this off!" I know that's probably the way I would have been thinking! Then God had the nerve to tell Gideon that his numbers were too great, and that his company needed to be smaller, so they couldn't say that their hands gave them the victory.

The first separation of the masses came at the place of fear. It was simple, really. There was no pep talk to try to get these guys pumped up. There was no back and forth trying to convince these men to do the right thing. It was simply stated to the company, "If you are fearful or afraid, you are free to go back from Gilead." When Gideon released this decree throughout the camp, 22,000 men left his company! Gideon quickly lost two thirds of his company in a moment. Gideon's response wasn't to condemn these men with a judgmental attitude. This didn't mean that they had rebelled against God and had fallen under a curse, it simply meant that they were afraid and God said they were free to go.

I know this is difficult to process for many, because zealous people want everyone to be just as zealous as they are. Hardcore worshipers want everyone to worship at the same level they do. The same can be said for intercessors, business people, dancers, artists and more. There is a great difference between being for someone, and being against someone. We each have people in our lives that are for us, but some of them are fearful of the battle we are called to. The difficult truth is that we are in greater danger when we have more people fighting alongside us who are afraid. We have greater success with fewer people, who are ordained to walk with us and are called to the same fight as we are.

Is There Not A Cause?

David also dealt with the issue of fear when it came to the Israelite army. We all know the story of when he went to take provisions to his brothers and encountered Goliath shouting insults at the nation and God of Israel. The entire scenario is fascinating, concerning this passage of Scripture. I believe it is important to note, that where this famous fight took place, was on land owned by the tribe of Judah. The Philistine army camped in a place that was not their own, and offered the terms of engagement they felt would best benefit them. Who did the Philistines send out as their champion? They sent out a man taller than all the others. This is important to consider, because Israel had its own "head and shoulders man" when it came to their king. The giant of the Philistines had hoped to fight the giant of the Israelites.

1 Samuel 9:2-
...a choice young man, and a goodly: and there was not among
the children of Israel a goodlier person than he: from his
*shoulders and upward **he was higher** than any of the people.*
(KJV) (Emphasis Mine)

The Philistine giant emerged onto the battlefield and began to intimidate the Israelites in whatever way he could think of. Where was the great giant of the Israelites? King Saul was hiding in his tent. The men of the Israelite army had fear in their hearts because of the sights and sounds of Goliath. The stakes of the proposed encounter were tremendous! The challenge was a one on one fight, and to the victor would go the spoils of war. No one in Israel had the guts to face Goliath, until now. What was it about David that made him have no fear in the face of this giant among men?

In 1 Samuel 17 we see this encounter unfold. Where things start getting interesting is when we see the reward that king Saul offered to the one who would stand against Goliath. The reward for the one who kills Goliath is generous and includes: great riches, Saul's daughter in marriage, and any debt of the house of David's father paid in full. These prizes were great, but David was motivated by something that went far beyond riches and women. David had a question in his heart that drove him to face Goliath.

1 Samuel 17:29-
*And David said, What have I now done? **Is there not a cause?***
(KJV) (Emphasis Mine)

Is there not a cause? The answer to this powerful question will move you beyond fear! What was the cause that was worth defending at this moment in history? Could the cause be the covenant made with Noah, or perhaps with Abraham? Could it be the promises made to Moses and the nation of Israel that stirred the heart of David? Maybe what stirred David was the more recent history of Joshua and Caleb coming into the Promised Land. The Philistines were nothing new, but this moment, when David faced Goliath, was about to change everything. David found courage and strength in the "presence" and "promises" of God. Goliath was killed at the hands of David and the Israelite army overtook the Philistines that day.

> David found courage and strength in the "presence" and "promises" of God.

GUARANTEED
VICTORY

CHAPTER THREE
THE SPIRIT OF FEAR

2 Timothy 1:7-
For God hath not given us the spirit of fear; but of power, and of love, and of a sound mind. (KJV)

The word for "spirit" in the above verse is *pneuma* and means "the soul or vital spirit." In other words, this verse is not telling us to engage in spiritual warfare against a spirit called "fear", but it's addressing the type of soul or vital spirit that God has given to us. Let me be clear, I do not believe that fear is a spirit that tries to attack us. I believe instead, that fear is the result of a systematic breakdown of the understanding of who we are in the family of God. Fear is not part of the covenant that God made with His Son. Jesus walked in full assurance of Who He was even when He journeyed to the cross. He didn't endure the cross with fear looming over Him, but rather He endured hardship for the joy that was set before him (Heb. 12:2). The joy of the Lord is our strength (Neh. 8:10)!

Our souls and spirits are designed to function without fear as a contaminant. Since God hasn't given us the spirit of fear, what has He given us? God has given us power, love, and a sound mind. These three qualities are the foundation stones for optimal living in the Kingdom of God. They are also vitally connected to the proper understanding of our identity as sons and daughters. The sad truth is that religion has manufactured more fear than anything else! The religious church, in particular, is one of the greatest institutions of fear known to mankind. We are created to live lives free from fear, but are taught to be afraid, many times at the instant of our personal salvation.

> The religious church, in particular, is one of the greatest institutions of fear known to mankind.

The religious church has created a climate of fear by keeping the saints of God in an Old Covenant mindset. This mindset extends towards God, one another, and infiltrates the values we develop throughout the course of our lives. This type of lifestyle produces a judgmental God Who is ready, at a moments notice, to punish us for our failures and mistakes. It causes us to indulge in self condemnation and empowers the cycles of sin and failure that we try so desperately to escape from. If God were truly angry with us, then we would have sufficient reason to be afraid. The truth is that God is not angry with us, and we find abundant proof of this truth in the life and ministry of Jesus.

Know The Truth

> *John 8:32-*
> *Then you will know the truth, and the truth will set you free. (NIV)*

I have heard this verse quoted and taught more times than I can recall. What will really change how you apply this verse to your life is when you consider who Jesus was talking to when He said this. He was speaking to the Jews of His day. These were people that were well versed in the law; they knew it and practiced it zealously. Even though they were performing what was "right", they still had no freedom in their lives. They held themselves to a standard that was impossible to meet and therefore, the standard kept them oppressed, bound, and full of fear.

Jesus expressed to them that the only way they would be free, was by hearing the truth. This is amazing! He was, in essence, saying that the law you adhere to so closely does not contain the truth that makes men free. The truth Jesus spoke of was grace. When you have an encounter with the grace and love of God, any fear, guilt, condemnation, and addictions you struggle with will fall away.

John 1:17-
For the law was given through Moses; grace and truth came through Jesus Christ. (NIV)

Why doesn't this verse read, "the *law and truth* came through Moses; *grace* and *truth* came through Jesus Christ"? Hear this carefully, the only truth that is found in the law is the truth that binds you. 1 Corinthians 15:56 tells us that the power of sin is the law! The law was never meant to make us free; it was established to show us how desperate our state as humanity was outside of the grace and mercy of God. This is why it is impossible to mix law and grace. It cannot work! This was one of the primary problems that the Galatians struggled with. They received the word by faith, but then tried to continue in the works of the law or the flesh to be made perfect.

Galatians 3:6-13-
Even as Abraham believed God, and it was accounted to him for righteousness. Know ye therefore that they which are of faith, the same are the children of Abraham. And the scripture, foreseeing that God would justify the heathen through faith, preached before the gospel unto Abraham, saying, In thee shall all nations be blessed. So then they which be of faith are blessed with faithful Abraham. For as many as are of the works of the law are under the curse: for it is written, Cursed is every one that

continueth not in all things which are written in the book of the law to do them. But that no man is justified by the law in the sight of God, it is evident: for, The just shall live by faith. And the law is not of faith: but, The man that doeth them shall live in them. Christ hath redeemed us from the curse of the law, being made a curse for us: for it is written, Cursed is every one that hangeth on a tree (KJV)

The covenant and promises made to Abraham were outside of the law! Abraham had been dead 430 years before the law was given to Moses. In short, the curse (any curse) that was destined to be a part of your life, is cured and remedied by the sacrifice of Jesus. He actually ratified the covenant God made with Abraham and caused it to be a part of your life through Himself. The law was instituted because of transgression, but was fulfilled through the life and death of Jesus.

Jesus loves you! He doesn't hold your mistakes against you. He is not here to judge anyone, but to save all who would call upon Him. It is this truth that breaks down prison walls and causes our wrong believing to die away. During His earthly ministry, those who were imperfect, weren't afraid that Jesus was going to condemn or judge them. He actually was harshest to those who thought they were perfect in their own minds. The "religious" god created by the religious exercises of men, is not the real God! The true God is One of infinite grace. He resists the proud and religious, but empowers the hurting and the humble.

The true God is One of infinite grace.

The Power Of Adoption

> *Romans 8:15-*
> *For you did not receive the spirit of slavery to fall back into fear, but you have received the Spirit of adoption as sons, by whom we cry, "Abba! Father!" (ESV)*

Slavery (bondage) and fear go hand in hand. This is why it is simply not enough to "cope" with your issues. No one has the power to simultaneously thrive in life and carry all of their issues with them. Perhaps addictions keep you fearful today. Maybe past offenses and abuses continue to rule your relationships with fear. For many of us, trying to have a law-based relationship with God and others is about to drive us to insanity. Whatever issues you carry presently that have produced slavery and fear in your life, God wants to set you radically free!

God brings us His freedom as a gift. This gift is *adoption*. Once you believe and understand how the heavenly Father sovereignly and divinely adopted you, it will cause the chains of slavery to fall away forever. The Master doesn't adopt servants and expect them to grow up in an environment of slavery. No! Our Master has adopted us as His own and is greatly satisfied when we enjoy the fruit of His inheritance. We are the family of God, and we need not be fearful of Him.

> *Galatians 4:4-6-*
> *But when the fulness of the time was come, God sent forth his Son, made of a woman, made under the law, To redeem them that were under the law, that we might receive the adoption of sons. And because ye are sons, God hath sent forth the Spirit of his Son into your hearts, crying, Abba, Father. (KJV)*

Understand this, you will never thrive as a son or daughter of God if you approach Him based on the requirements of the law! Jesus came to earth so that He could establish the greatest and most successful adoption program in the history of mankind. When Jesus redeemed us, it wasn't from the claws of the devil. At best, the devil is defeated. Jesus came and redeemed us from the law! He established a new pattern for righteousness that is imputed to us the day we recognize Him as Savior and King. Our adoption as sons and daughters is only capable through the Grace of the Lord. Remember, His *grace is very sufficient*!

Jesus came to earth so that He could establish the greatest and most successful adoption program in the history of mankind.

GUARANTEED
VICTORY

CHAPTER FOUR
FLOWING IN POWER

God doesn't operate in terms of quantity, but He operates in terms of quality. Men and women of quality do not allow fear to contaminate their lives. They understand that they have not been given a spirit of fear, and therefore do not entertain the thoughts and actions associated with it. They are secure in their identity. They realize that they are well equipped by God, and they have not forgotten the cause of God for their lives and the nations of the earth. Like King David of old, their courage and confidence comes from the promises of God in motion.

The Church right now seems to be focused on receiving power from God, but is not so eager, it seems, to seek after the authority God has released to it. Maybe in our minds we believe that power is more important, but the truth is that power and authority are to be equally exercised in the life of the believer. Demonstrations of power may indeed draw people to recognize God, but it is authority (that comes from the goodness of God) that causes repentance and strengthens the foundations in order that we might be useful in the hands of the King. Remember, Jesus met with Moses (authority) and Elijah (power) when He was on the mount of transfiguration. (See my book *Becoming Glorious* to read about this dynamic in greater detail.)

power - *the ability to do or act*

authority - *the power to determine, adjudicate, or otherwise settle issues or disputes; rights delegated or given*

Many saints today have the ability to act on any number of issues, but few have the wisdom and understanding of the authority necessary to use power wisely. If you do not respect the empowerment you have, it can be easily abused. When someone hands you the keys to a car, you are instantly empowered to drive. That being said, if you have not been trained (understand the authority that comes with driving) properly, you will find out just how dangerous power without proper understanding of authority can be.

I feel that much of the harm done by the saints today is the result of acting like they have a license, when all they have at this point, is a permit. When you initially receive your drivers permit, you must still have someone licensed in the vehicle with you. I know the terminology I am using is simple, but it will help us in life. This is also a picture of what training and submission should like in the local church. Those who are babes in the Kingdom should willingly and joyfully submit to those who are seasoned in authority. True authority doesn't want to neglect or hold back anyone, but it does want to make sure they are seasoned, in order to use the authority that they have been given in an appropriate way.

As we progress in our understanding, the power and authority in our lives work together. This is a great mentoring principle. Think of the many potential leaders who have received powerful promises of God. If they are not careful, they believe that the promises automatically produce authority in their lives. Too many ministries are acting like they have been given the license from God to do what He promised they would, but the reality is that at this point, they have only been given a learners permit. When God gives you a promise, it is wise to connect with a leader in your life who understands authority. Young ministers need to connect to seasoned leaders who bear the proof of the authority of God in their lives and ministries.

The Need For Order

The fastest growing expressions of the Church right now are in the Charismatic, Pentecostal, and Non-Denominational movements. I believe these are seeing explosive growth because of the desire of God's people to flow in the gifts and fruits of the Spirit that He has provided for them. Personally, I have been exposed to the move of the Spirit for nearly my entire life, and started being trained in using the gifts in 1991. Over the many years of training and learning to be sensitive to the presence of the Lord, I have seen some of the most glorious encounters you can imagine.

Our ministry has been training people in operating in the gifts of the Spirit since 1993. We have established a reputation, as a house, that we carry a sure word from the Lord and we have trained thousands of people in how to flow in the supernatural. The vast majority of people have instant excitement when they are being trained for the first time in something they have never experienced before. Once they get some training in an area, their confidence begins to grow. As we began to see the training increase and more and more people begin to flow in confidence in the gifts, we also began to see the real need for guidelines and order to be established.

Don't run from the word *order*. Order is not a bad thing. The abuses of order are not good and they can greatly damage people, but I am talking about healthy order that allows the good things of God to thrive. Where the need for order became most prevalent in our ministry, was when we started having *Prophetic Activation* weekends. We would routinely train people in the prophetic, that had never been exposed to it before. They would get excited, rightly so, and would want to share this newly discovered gift with everyone they encountered. We began to hear that individuals would go to Wal-Mart, or a restaurant, and would begin prophesying to people. When people enquired about where they learned to do this, they would say, "Dominion Church International trained me in how to do this, and they anointed me as a prophet!" We knew we had to set some guidelines quick!

In our *Prophetic Activation* weekends we NEVER ordained anyone as prophets. We simply showed them how to flow in the gift of prophecy, that is available to all the saints. Along the lines of order, we asked those trained to submit their prophetic flow to their local house, to not fear to submit prophetic words to their eldership, to do their best to have their words recorded for the sake of posterity, and other such suggestions. We also asked people not to give "parking lot" prophecies, and to stay away from prophesying about marriages, babies, and major life decisions. Once we started using these guidelines, the people weren't squelched or put down. In fact, they thrived and were blessed even more.

The Gifts & Fruits Of The Spirit

When God birthed you into the earth, He also entrusted you with all kinds of great gifts. We have gifts that no amount of money can earn. I am not a man of any great business or political stature in the natural, but I have had the privilege of prophesying to the President of the United States and to two sitting state Governors. These didn't happen so I can boast of my own ability. My boast is in the Lord, and as long as I keep my ear on His heartbeat, He will bring my voice before the kings of the earth. God didn't design us to *think* our way through our lives, and simply do the best that we can. He designed us to be led by His Spirit and to be proficient with the gifts He has given us.

> *1 Corinthians 12:7-11-*
> *But the manifestation of the Spirit is given to every man to profit withal. For to one is given by the Spirit the word of wisdom; to another the word of knowledge by the same Spirit; To another faith by the same Spirit; to another the gifts of healing by the same Spirit; To another the working of miracles; to another prophecy; to another discerning of spirits; to another divers*

kinds of tongues; to another the interpretation of tongues: But all these worketh that one and the selfsame Spirit, dividing to every man severally as he will. (KJV)

We have a pretty impressive list of gifts that can operate in our lives. I liken the gifts of the Spirit to *power*. These gifts accomplish things that are not capable through human strength. As a son and daughter of the King, you can walk in supernatural wisdom, knowledge, faith, healings, prophecy, and more! How much would someone with cancer pay to be healed? What would someone give to have supernatural wisdom during the most difficult decision of their life? When mankind is in greatest need, you can release a manifestation of the Spirit of God in their lives and change it forever! God has given us many fantastic gifts, but He has also given us authority, that takes the use of these gifts in our lives, to a whole new level.

When mankind is in greatest need, you can release a manifestation of the Spirit of God in their lives and change it forever!

Galatians 5:22-23-
But the fruit of the Spirit is love, joy, peace, longsuffering, gentleness, goodness, faith, meekness, temperance: against such there is no law. (KJV)

When we discover the fruit of the Spirit, we begin to see how deep our foundation truly is. I liken the fruit of the Spirit to *authority*. I have seen people flowing powerfully in gifts and lacking greatly in fruit. When we walk in gifts without fruit, we can set ourselves up for some pretty dangerous results. The gifts of God flow very publicly, but the fruit of God is developed privately. It's hard to get much public buzz when you are ministering long-suffering, gentleness, and temperance, but these things will bring longevity and depth to the gifts of the Spirit.

The gifts and fruits of the Spirit are a match made in heaven! They show us the necessity for the marriage between power and authority. These two do not compete or threaten each other. They work together to produce well nourished and stable believers. Abiding in the presence of God, makes for fertile ground in the Spirit. Allow yourself to be caught up in Him, and you will see tremendous results.

The Second Separation

At this point, perhaps Gideon thought that there was still a chance of defeating the Midiantes with 10,000 men. Maybe some of his men were "closet" warriors, who had the ability to slay many adversaries and pick up the slack from the less experienced warriors. Surely this company of 10,000 was small enough for God to use against the countless masses of the Midianites! This is the point, where I'm not sure if I would want to hear God speak anymore or not, but alas, another separation was required by the Spirit of the Lord.

The second separation of the masses comes at the place of power. Power, in and of itself, can be a very dangerous thing, but knowing how to use the power that we have been given effectively, can change the world. Indeed, the Lord has invited us all to come into the place of power and authority, and when He does, let's be sure that our responses are wise ones.

> *Judges 7:4-7-*
> *And the Lord said unto Gideon, The people are yet too many; bring them down unto the water, and I will try them for thee there: and it shall be, that of whom I say unto thee, This shall go with thee, the same shall go with thee; and of whomsoever I say unto thee, This shall not go with thee, the same shall not go. So he brought down the people unto the water: and the Lord said unto Gideon, Every one that lappeth of the water with his tongue, as a dog lappeth, him shalt thou set by himself; likewise every one that boweth down upon his knees to drink. And the number of them that lapped, putting their hand to their mouth, were three hundred men: but all the rest of the people bowed down upon their knees to drink water. And the Lord said unto Gideon, By the three hundred men that lapped will I save you, and deliver the Midianites into thine hand: and let all the other people go every man unto his place. (KJV)*

When the thought of water came into the minds of 10,000 men that were hot and thirsty, you had better believe that a cool river of water looked like heaven on earth! Throw in the good possibility that these guys were most likely dressed in battle array, which included thick leather, and armament at some level, let's just say that these guys were not hot like guys in the sun with shorts and a t-shirt, but they were most likely sweltering in the heat of the day. The invitation to drink is welcomed, and the masses go down to drink from the river. Of the masses 9,700 get on their hands and knees to drink! They dunked their faces in, and drank without reservation, and cooled and refreshed themselves in abundance.

I once heard Dr. Kelley Varner teach of this encounter and that it could be likened, in one sense, to how saints respond to the river of the Holy Spirit. The first and largest separation of the saints comes in the outer court (Passover), and the second separation comes in the inner court (Pentecost), where the river is flowing freely to all who come. The difference we find here, is that there are those who drink from the river in two distinctively different ways. First, there are those who drink without reservation. You may think this is harmless enough, but when God has called you to attention, this is not the time to be face first in the water. Second, we find those who took the water into their hands and brought it up to their mouths. They drew from the cool and refreshing river, yet remained alert and ready for the task at hand.

It is of great importance for us to understand how to properly handle power and authority. I enjoy the party, that can be the Holy Spirit as much as anyone else, but I also want to be aware and available for service when God has called me to attention. There is plenty of water to go around. Those who are mature in God, know how to bring the water up to their mouths, but those who are not, get on all fours and enjoy without staying focused on what God has called them to. I am not against enjoying the presence of the Holy Spirit! But how many people have we affected negatively by taking the "super soaker" approach to sharing the Kingdom with them? A taste is sufficient to entice people into the fullness of God.

Psalm 34:8-
*O **taste and see** that the Lord is good: blessed is the man that*
trusteth in him. (KJV)(Emphasis Mine)

I believe that it was the proper understanding of authority that led Gideon's 300 to remain useful on the day of drinking. As much as they desired refreshing and the quenching of their thirst, they took their responsibility as warriors more seriously. God is always on the lookout for such faithful men and women. He knows that He can use us when we are called to do things that no one else has done, and say things that no one else has said. If we will commit to walk the disciplined path between power and authority, we will witness victories that few ever have!

If we will commit to walk in the disciplined path between power and authority, we will witness victories that few ever have!

Who Is In Charge?

The Father is truly in charge. I do not want that to come across as a cliché, but I want to communicate the gut-wrenching reality of this truth. The Church of this age is faced with one of the great truths of eternity: God is King and He has always been King. He is the King of the saint and sinner, the bound and the free, the rich and the poor, the ignorant and the educated, everyone. God does not have to be recognized, honored, followed or even loved, and He still remains sovereign. If you truly love the Father, this line of thought is exciting and full of life, but those who do not understand the truths of His Kingship can become greatly offended.

Those who desire to be in control, have fought the greatest battle found in chronological time. This desire has manifested in many different ways. It has been fought among religions, ethnic groups, social groups, political groups and others. Man has always wanted to be in control, and much blood has been spilt to that end. As convincing as men may be in arguing that what they do is for the cause of freedom, the truth is, that most of it is done out of the lust for power and control. Man, in his Adamic state, can only experience power through force. The greater frustration in this pursuit is that, no matter who wins, the victory is always temporary. There is a better way.

> *Proverbs 29:2 -*
> *When the [uncompromisingly] righteous are in authority, the*
> *people rejoice; but when the wicked man rules, the people*
> *groan and sigh. (AMP)*

Adamic mankind misunderstands the concept of true rulership. Real authority is not defined by military strength or mental suave; true power is only extended in and through the righteousness of Christ. This power was granted to the Lord by God Himself (Daniel 7:14; John 17:1-3) and is consummated in the Body of Christ corporately (Matthew 28:18-19). This rulership flows out of righteousness, which is both authored and finished by Him. This power is not lorded over a people, in order to force submission upon them; this authority empowers people to live by the faith and love of Jesus Himself. Where the righteous rule (Jesus and the corporate Christ), the people rejoice!

There are a people in the earth who desire more of God! They have loved Him as **Savior** in the Feast of Passover, as **Teacher** in the Feast of Pentecost, and now they are pursuing strongly after Him as **King** in the Feast of Tabernacles. The plumb line, who is Jesus, has the preeminence in this place above all else (Colossians 1:18). The pattern of Jesus is full of the abundance of life in the Spirit, and His pattern also bears the greatest destruction for the flesh of Adam. Jesus is the One above all, and what He has accomplished in the scope of all things spiritual, as well as natural, cannot be challenged or outdone! Greater is He!

> *I John 4:4-*
> *Ye are of God, little children, and have overcome them:*
> *because greater is he that is in you, than he that is in the*
> *world. (KJV)*

GUARANTEED
VICTORY

CHAPTER FIVE
THE HIGH MOUNTAINS

Gideon sent out a call for anyone to assemble who would fight against the Midianites. The Lord told Gideon that the victory would be His, but He didn't give Gideon any details as to how it would happen. The masses that gathered together to face the Midianites, numbered 32,000 men. This may sound like a large number, but compared to the several hundred thousand Midianites, the odds were not good. Just when Gideon thought, "Maybe this could work with these guys", the plan of God kicked into high gear. God told Gideon that his number (32,000 men – with odds of 6 to 1) was too many. He instructed Gideon to tell those who were afraid that they were free to go. When this happened, 22,000 men left. The first separation was at the place of fear.

Now Gideon was feeling the pressure like never before. Perhaps he had some time to regain his thoughts, and started trying to figure out how in the world God would defeat the Midianites with only 10,000 men. Perhaps, at this point Gideon thought, "He is a God of miracles. This could still work." God then reveals to Gideon that his number (10,000 men – with odds of 19 to 1) was yet too many. He instructed Gideon to send his masses down to the river to drink. God gave clarification to Gideon of who he should call out to use for His purposes. The number that remained that God could use was 300 men. The second separation was at the place of power.

Judges 7:7-8-
And the LORD said unto Gideon, By the three hundred men that
lapped will I save you, and deliver the Midianites into thine
hand: and let all the other people go every man unto his place.
So the people took victuals in their hand, and their trumpets: and
he sent all the rest of Israel every man unto his tent, and retained
those three hundred men: and the host of Midian was beneath
him in the valley. (KJV)

Those who are of the quality of the 300 must answer the invitation to ascend. It is interesting that the separations of fear and power came in an ascended place. Judges 7:8 reveals to us that the encampment of the Midianites was beneath Gideon and his men in the valley. The 32,000 men that were separated from the camp of Gideon had no revelation of where they were. They had the vantage point all along! Whoever has the higher ground will always have the advantage. It is from this perspective, that we begin to see the plan and purpose of God unfold in ways we could have never imagined.

Whoever has the higher ground will always have the advantage.

The Ascended Place

Have you ever seen a situation from higher ground? From an ascended perspective, everything we encounter is vastly different. You are able to see the plain ahead of you more clearly. You are, often times, able to see the end of a matter, while you are still in the middle of it. You are able to plan and strategize more effectively, because you can see what is coming from a greater distance. Life in the kingdom of God is the high life! We are seated with Christ in heavenly places, and are equipped to live life with the greatest perspective known to humanity.

> *Ephesians 2:6-*
> *...and raised us up with him and seated us with him in the*
> *heavenly places in Christ Jesus. (ESV)*

Jesus always has an ascended perspective. This is what fueled the unique qualities of His earthly ministry. He was able to see things as they truly were, and not what face value offered. The high perspective allowed Jesus to see healing instead of blindness. The proper perspective allowed Him to see abundance instead of hunger. From the heavenly perspective, Jesus was able to see the old passing away, as the new was being birthed in the earth. Many may think, "Sure, Jesus had the right perspective, but I am not Jesus." Jesus is not simply an unattainable figure, He is our divine pattern. Since Jesus has an ascended perspective, so can we!

> Jesus was able to see the old passing away, as the new was being birthed in the earth.

Our Lord extends to us a continual invitation to ascend and sit with Him. This is already true positionally, but we must receive it as truth experientially. The bulk of the frustrations that believers encounter in life, is because of the disconnect between what God says about them, and what they perceive as truth in the moment. It is difficult to believe that we are seated with Christ in heavenly places when we feel like we are in the dumps. As it is with most things in the Kingdom of God, we must accept the invitation to live and think differently, by faith.

> *Romans 1:17-*
> *For therein is the righteousness of God revealed from faith to*
> *faith: as it is written, The just shall live by faith. (KJV)*

Embracing our God ordained perspective is imperatively connected to faith. In truth, it impacts every area of our lives in God. The Father not only births in us "foundational" faith, but He also ministers to us "finishing" faith. This spiritual equipping takes us above the everyday smog of life, and allows us to shake off the non-essentials that so easily distract us. It also challenges us to start flourishing in what faith is really all about. Those who live the ascended life don't think in terms of what their faith can help them to gain, but instead, they seek God as to what faith really accomplishes.

The entire company that Gideon had in his command (32,000 men), were already in a high place. The problem was, the bulk of them had no idea where they were. Even though they had the high ground, they were still full of fear. The company of Gideon was high above their enemies, but they still had no understanding of their power. Said and done, only Gideon and his 300 remained in the mountains surrounding the Midianites. It's from the high places that Gideon begins to receive perspective that changes everything.

The Dreams Of Enemies

Now that 300 men were what remained of Gideon's army, there was no doubt an increase of anxiety in Gideon. When He saw the warriors he was left with, the Lord woke him in the night and had him go and survey the Midianites more closely. God instructs Gideon to go down and get close to the camp, so that he could hear what was in the mouths of the encampment of his adversaries. Can you see this picture in your mind? Gideon and Phurah are descending into the camp of a multitude without number.

> *Judges 7:9-12-*
> *And it came to pass the same night, that the LORD said unto him, Arise, get thee down unto the host; for I have delivered it into thine hand. But if thou fear to go down, go thou with Phurah thy servant down to the host: And thou shalt hear what they say; and afterward shall thine hands be strengthened to go down unto the host. Then went he down with Phurah his servant unto the outside of the armed men that were in the host. And the Midianites and the Amalekites and all the children of the east lay along in the valley like grasshoppers for multitude; and their camels were without number, as the sand by the sea side for multitude. (KJV)*

This scene would have been enough to take the courage from anyone. As Gideon surveyed the vast company of men, he realized the odds were worse than he had ever thought! Even in the best case scenario, with his company of 300, each man would be outnumbered 667 to 1! We are not told what went through Gideon's mind in this moment. We know he was afraid, because he came down to the camp with Phurah, but we have no idea what else was going through his mind. We see a discouraging scene at the campside of the Midianites, but then something very interesting happens. In the moment when fear should be at its pinnacle, Gideon begins to hear of the dreams of his enemies.

> *Judges 7:13-14-*
> *And when Gideon was come, behold, there was a man that told a*
> *dream unto his fellow, and said, Behold, I dreamed a dream,*
> *and, lo, a cake of barley bread tumbled into the host of Midian,*
> *and came unto a tent, and smote it that it fell, and overturned it,*
> *that the tent lay along. And his fellow answered and said, This is*
> *nothing else save the sword of Gideon the son of Joash, a man of*
> *Israel: for into his hand hath God delivered Midian, and all the*
> *host. (KJV)*

Fear is toxic. In the moment Gideon heard the dream of a Midianite, he began to understand why fear could not be in his camp. If it were, all the 32,000 men at his charge, would have been trampled underfoot. When fear is in your heart, you will prophesy your own demise. God will use a cake of barley bread (representing common men of Israel) to roll into your camp of warriors and dignitaries, and strike your tent (your habitation, your place of war strategies) to gain the victory! God removed fear from the camp of Gideon because it would be a key component evident in the camp of the Midiantes. Because of fear, the army of the Midiantes had lost before there was ever a fight.

When fear is in your heart, you will prophesy your own demise.

As Gideon's perspective changed, he began to see the host of Midian for what they truly were. This was not an army full of fearless warriors, who eat the flesh of giants. No, they were riddled with fear, and had a sense that God was with Israel. They were so afraid, that even the thought of war against Gideon had them on edge. I cannot downplay the importance of right perspective when it comes to our lives in God! When you see as God sees, you can have what God has. In this case, God had already secured the victory for Gideon and his men.

GUARANTEED
VICTORY

CHAPTER SIX
WARRIORS OF WORSHIP

What is worship? What compels us to worship? I have heard worship taught on for most of my life, and I still have the feeling that we miss its value most of the time. The importance of worship is seen thoroughly throughout Scripture. Worship is real, raw, powerful, personal, and relational. That being said, for a lot of saints, it's just part of how you open a Sunday service. Worship must be a lifestyle, and it is of great importance that we see this quality in Gideon emerge at just the right time.

Judges 7:15-
*And it was so, when Gideon heard the telling of the dream, and the interpretation thereof, **that he worshipped**, and returned into the host of Israel, and said, Arise; for the LORD hath delivered into your hand the host of Midian. (KJV) (Emphasis Mine)*

The word for "worship" in the above verse is *wayyistahu* and it means "to bow down to the earth." Why is this expression of worship vital for us to grasp? Physically, it is the act of getting on ones hands and knees and putting our face into the ground. This posture allows the worshiper to do something of utmost importance; it allows him to get his heart above his head. I know that there are various expressions of worship, but I believe this one is the most sincere before God. This posture takes the mind out of the equation and shows the Lord the true intentions of the heart. If you can figure out how to worship God in the face of your greatest obstacles, you will walk in the life of guaranteed victory.

As soon as Gideon heard that the Midianites were afraid of him and his company, Gideon worshiped. He could have done any number of things when he heard this joyous news. He could've instantly gone to his captains and planned the attack. He could've reviewed the odds and recalculated their chances. Gideon didn't defer to his "head mode" when he heard of the intervention of God. He immediately shifted into his "heart mode". His heart before God was what was of greatest value, and it was the hearts of his 300 men that God would ultimately use to defeat the Midianite host.

What Is Worship?

I believe that worship is the thankful acknowledgment and interaction with the presence of God. I have no desire to compartmentalize my worship of the King. I want my worship to be sincere and continual. It is vital for the believer to remain in constant awareness and thanksgiving concerning the presence of God. We should be aware of God during work, play, eating, shopping, and at any other time. Our awareness of the presence of God cannot be confined to mental recognition, but it is most genuinely experienced when it is birthed within the heart.

> *John 4:24-*
> *God is a Spirit: and they that worship him must worship him in spirit and in truth. (KJV)*

Did you now that worship is not part of the lifestyle of all believers? In John 4 the phrase, "they that worship", indicates that not everyone worships God. This is not addressing those in darkness, this applies to those who are already in the light. Those who have a "worship deficiency" lack peace, and live much of their lives in confusion. Not everyone worships, because worship does not come naturally, but it is something that is cultivated, and it should become a discipline in our lives. The more we create an environment of the purposeful thanksgiving of Who God is, the greater and more fulfilling our expression of worship will become.

> Those who have a "worship deficiency" lack peace, and live much of their lives in confusion.

Warriors are trained in atmospheres of worship. I know this sounds strange, since most people equate worship with solemn harmonies and orchestral strings. How can worship forge warriors? David is a prime example of how warriors are born in the place of worship. David would watch the sheep of his father in the open field, and he would worship and slay. He would worship the King, and he would slay the lion and the bear. Where did the boy David get the skill to slay such formidable beasts? He gained supernatural courage and confidence during his times of heart worship before the Lord!

> *Romans 12:1-2-*
> *I appeal to you therefore, brothers, by the mercies of God, to present your bodies as a living sacrifice, holy and acceptable to God, which is your spiritual worship. Do not be conformed to this world, but be transformed by the renewal of your mind, that by testing you may discern what is the will of God, what is good and acceptable and perfect. (ESV)*

As our understanding of worship unfolds, we begin to see how all encompassing it is meant to be in our lives. The whole of our bodies and our lives, are to be given unto the Lord in worship. Authentic worship keeps us from the desire to conform to the world. When our focus remains on the pure and powerful presence of God, we have no need to focus on the lesser things. There also a direct connection between a lifestyle of worship and having our minds renewed. The more we meditate on the presence of God (His glory, goodness, mercy, kindness, love, and more…), the more our mind is renewed unto the mind of Christ.

Philippians 4:8-
Finally, brothers, whatever is true, whatever is honorable,
whatever is just, whatever is pure, whatever is lovely,
whatever is commendable, if there is any excellence, if there
is anything worthy of praise, think about these things. (ESV)

Love That Compels

God's love for you is unconditional! This love cannot be earned. This love has nothing to do with what you do or don't do, but it has to do with how God sees and receives you. You are His beloved. The emphasis throughout the old covenant focused more on our love for God, but the new covenant emphasizes and focuses on God's love for us! The love of God is magnetic and it compels all who receive it to desire to reciprocate. God gives love without requirement, and this is the primary reason His love is so compelling.

Psalm 121:2-8-
My help comes from the Lord, who made heaven and earth. He
will not let your foot be moved; he who keeps you will not
slumber.Behold, he who keeps Israel will neither slumber nor
sleep. The Lord is your keeper; the Lord is your shade on your
right hand.The sun shall not strike you by day, nor the moon by
night. The Lord will keep you from all evil; he will keep your life.
The Lord will keep your going out and your coming in from this
time forth and forevermore. (ESV)

How are we worthy to receive such love and blessing from God? The answer is simply, because of Jesus. Everything we receive from God is given to us as we find ourselves totally enveloped in His perfect sacrifice. It was Jesus Who cleansed us from all sin. It was Jesus who became a curse for us. It was Jesus who brought a new covenant of grace and life. When God looks at us now, He only sees Jesus! He doesn't see who you once were, He doesn't even remember who you once were. He sees someone righteous, blessed, and full of favor.

1 John 4:7-15-
Beloved, let us love one another: for love is of God; and
every one that loveth is born of God, and knoweth God. He
that loveth not knoweth not God; for God is love. In this was
manifested the love of God toward us, because that God sent
his only begotten Son into the world, that we might live
through him. Herein is love, not that we loved God, but that
he loved us, and sent his Son to be the propitiation for our
sins. Beloved, if God so loved us, we ought also to love one
another. No man hath seen God at any time. If we love one
another, God dwelleth in us, and his love is perfected in us.
Hereby know we that we dwell in him, and he in us, because
he hath given us of his Spirit. And we have seen and do testify
that the Father sent the Son to be the Saviour of the world.
Whosoever shall confess that Jesus is the Son of God, God
dwelleth in him, and he in God. (KJV)

These verses paint a beautiful picture of the grace of God concerning humanity. The greatest manifestation of love that God ever showed, was when He sent His only begotten Son into the world, that we might live through Him. It also explains that real love was not found in "us loving God", but instead, in "God loving us". We are further instructed that the more we are exposed to the love of God, that it creates an environment in which we should be able to love one another. This is where holiness is birthed in the life of the believer. If you are not seeing holiness manifested in your life, it is due to a love deficiency! Where? The deficiency is the result of not understanding the love God has for you!

1 John 4:16-19-
And we have known and believed the love that God hath to us.
God is love; and he that dwelleth in love dwelleth in God, and
God in him. Herein is our love made perfect, that we may have
boldness in the day of judgment: because as he is, so are we in
this world. There is no fear in love; but perfect love casteth out
fear: because fear hath torment. He that feareth is not made
*perfect in love. **We love him, because he first loved us.** (KJV)*
(Emphasis Mine)

God's love for you, should eventually produce your love for God. So many are desperate to love God, but have no understanding of His love for them. This is why much of their lives are so frustrating and dualistic. The only love we can have for God, is birthed out of believing and receiving His love for us. This is why there is such a great importance in living a lifestyle of worship. The more you are exposed to the presence of God, the greater your love for Him will grow and flourish.

> The more you are exposed to the presence of God, the greater your love for Him will grow and flourish.

GUARANTEED
VICTORY

CHAPTER SEVEN
THE WEAPONS OF WAR

I want to preface at the start of this chapter, some of my personal beliefs concerning spiritual warfare. I believe that spiritual warfare in the life of the believer, is one of the most misunderstood dynamics of the Christian life. I also feel that the vast majority of what is espoused as spiritual warfare, is the taking of little information offered in Scripture, and then taking that information to places that are fueled by wild speculation. It is my belief that most of what we label "spiritual warfare", is most likely the real war that is waged in the mindsets of men.

Don't dismiss this chapter, after reading the first paragraph. I simply try to maintain my focus on the overwhelmingly supported themes of

Scripture. A principle I was taught many years ago has saved me from wasting valuable time in my pursuit of truth. That principle is: where the Bible says little, say little, and where the Bible says much, say much. Think about it, in the whole of Scripture, how much focus is given to darkness and us warring with principalities and powers? I am not a coward when it comes to this subject, I am simply saying little where only little is said.

In Scripture, I see an overwhelming amount of evidence that focuses on the finished work of Jesus. I see multiple passages that talk about the saints walking in the fullness of victory. I see lots of places where our identity is described as rulers and princes. If you connect the dots of what is heavily supported in Scripture concerning our identity in Christ, the way you view warfare and resistance in the spirit, will radically shift. We do not war to win. We war because we have already won! By this, I mean we are the divine occupational force in the earth. Our King has spoiled the adversaries in our midst, and our primary purpose today, is to bring continued acknowledgment of His Lordship to the ends of the earth.

I personally believe that the area of warfare, along with everything else in our walk with God, must be connected to our obedience. Obedience to God is always our safety net. If God tells me to pray about something, I pray. If God tells me to war against something, I war. I don't make these things primary themes in life just because someone else tells me that they should be. I have found however, that as my focus and understanding of God, my identity, and my empowerment changes, so does how and what I hear from God. Gideon understood that obedience was the key to his guaranteed victory, and it is the key to our victory as well.

> We do not war to win. We war because we have already won!

Where Are The Swords?

After Gideon saw fear in the camp of the Midianites, he worshiped the Lord. This act of worship got his heart above his head. Worship cleared the air for Gideon, and between the time he worshiped and got back to his camp, he had received his orders from the Lord. The

Lord shared a unique plan with Gideon, and the weapons of war that were assigned, weren't what men would choose, especially to engage in war against a countless army. What were the secret weapons of Gideon's warfare? The weapons of his warfare were pitchers, lamps, and trumpets. When Gideon called his men and equipped them with pitchers, lamps (torches), and trumpets, these items were literal, but they also have great spiritual significance for the life of the believer. Over the next few pages, I would like to look at the significance of these weapons, and how they each are vital in the life of the believer.

> *Judges 7:16-18-*
> *And he divided the three hundred men into three companies, and he put a trumpet in every man's hand, with empty pitchers, and lamps within the pitchers. And he said unto them, Look on me, and do likewise: and, behold, when I come to the outside of the camp, it shall be that, as I do, so shall ye do. When I blow with a trumpet, I and all that are with me, then blow ye the trumpets also on every side of all the camp, and say, The sword of the LORD, and of Gideon. (KJV)*

The Pitcher

The pitchers that Gideon's company carried, were made of clay. They were not decorative or ornamental. They were utilities that were necessary for daily living. They used them for the transport and storage of water. They also used them for transport and usage of food. They were versatile and common, and there were lots of them. The Lord didn't simply instruct the 300 to arm themselves with what was readily available, but He required vessels that would serve a purpose that they never had before.

> *2 Corinthians 4:7-*
> *But we have this treasure in jars of clay, to show that the surpassing power belongs to God and not to us. (ESV)*

I believe these pitchers are an accurate picture of who we are. We may not seem very ornamental or decorative at times, but we are greatly useful. The truth is, the treasure we carry on the inside, cannot be seen by outward appearances. We carry treasure in ourselves, the greatest treasure of all! We carry within us the fullness of the Godhead. We actually prefer when people underestimate us, because it only gives us greater occasions to give God all the more glory. This may be radical for you to hear, but you are a weapon! You carry the greatest light that dispels darkness. You carry the greatest force of victory that mankind has ever known. Within you, is the ability to call storms to cease. Within you, is the ability to call an end to violence and injustice. Within you, is the love that transforms the hearts of men, and the goodness of God that causes them to repent. Your usefulness as a vessel of the King, is at an all time high!

> Within you, is the love that transforms the hearts of men, and the goodness of God that causes them to repent.

When Gideon heard the dream of the Midianite, we find that the man saw a loaf of barley bread roll into the camp, and the loaf struck the tent. There are two truths that we must not miss from this dream. First, the barley loaf was common bread. This meant that God would not need elite men of war to overtake the Midianites. All God would need was the common men of Israel to gain the victory. Secondly, the barley loaf struck the tent. This truth is a little more subtle. The Midianite shared from his dream, that *THE* tent was struck, not *A* tent. He was referring to a special tent. He was most likely, referring to the tent of the King or highly seated officials within the camp of Midian. This is why there was so much fear in the Midianite camp. They feared that even the common men (barley) amongst Israel, would easily strike down the best they had to offer in war.

The Lamps or Torches

Gideon handed his men empty pitchers with lamps inside. The imagery here is simple to grasp. Again, we see a picture of who Christ is in us. The lamp is the light of the Lord. He is the treasure that is hidden in us. He continually burns on the inside of us, and when He gets hotter, is when we have more of a desire for Him to be seen. The pitcher must conceal Him at first, but as we mature in

Him, He is purposed to be publicly displayed for all to see and know Him.

Matthew 5:16-
Let your light so shine before men, that they may see your good works, and glorify your Father which is in heaven. (KJV)

When we release the light of Christ, it serves as a beacon to the people of the world that draws them to the Father in heaven. This is not something that we strive to attain, but it is a part of who we are as the sons and daughters of the King. We must find the best ways for the light to shine. One of the greatest ways that we find in Scripture for the light to shine, is by taking it up to a high place. The higher the light is, the greater the impact it will make. This also speaks to our invitation to ascend and to pursue seeing and living from a new perspective.

Matthew 5:14-15-
Ye are the light of the world. A city that is set on a hill cannot be hid. Neither do men light a candle, and put it under a bushel, but on a candlestick; and it giveth light unto all that are in the house. (KJV)

We must never forget that light shines best in the darkest places. These torches that Gideon's men carried pierced the darkness of the night. This was the only sight that the Midianites witnessed at their defeat. Can you imagine seeing piercing light in the midst of the darkness of night around the mountain tops that surrounded their valley? When these lights came out of hiding from their jars of clay, they caused the eyes of their enemies to be blinded with a fear and awe that they had never experienced before.

The Trumpet

The third weapon that Gideon's 300 possessed, was a trumpet. Of course, we understand that the trumpet produces sound. The sound it makes is distinct, sharp, and loud. One trumpet alone can be hard to handle in close proximity, but 300 trumpets that are blowing in unison, create a deafening wave of frequency that would be very intimidating to behold. Add to the fact that this amplified sound was released in the night without warning, it could have sounded like 300,000 trumpets when the Midianites were awakened in terror by them.

There is a unique relationship between God and sound. When Scripture first introduces our heavenly Father, He is speaking. There is creativity locked up in the sounds of God. There are a multitude of verses that teach us the importance of speaking, singing, shouting, prophesying, and decreeing. It makes sense, when you think about it. God loves sound, and His kids love sound too.

The Voice Of A Trumpet

John the beloved probably had the most experience with the dynamic of a voice sounding like a trumpet. When he was receiving the revelation of Christ, there were multiple times that he heard voices that sounded as trumpets. What does this mean? The voice of a trumpet signifies to the hearer, this is important to listen to. The voice of the trumpet releases a loud, clear, and concise sound. When you hear the voice of a trumpet, there is no missing what was said, and nothing is lost in translation.

> *Revelation 1:10-*
> *I was in the Spirit on the Lord's day, and heard behind me a great voice, as of a trumpet (KJV)*

> *Revelation 4:1-*
> *After this I looked, and, behold, a door was opened in heaven: and the first voice which I heard was as it were of a trumpet talking with me; which said, Come up hither, and I will shew thee things which must be hereafter. (KJV)*

The sound that God is calling us to release today, is as that of a trumpet. For too long the church has been making uncertain sounds. Could it be that we have not been heard because of our doubts, insecurities, fear, and anxiety? As we mature in our understanding of who we are in God, the sound that we release should become all the more certain. The voices of the saints are not meant to be that of tepid droplets of water, but of the sound of many waters that announce the strength and surety of the heart of the Prince of Peace!

As we mature in our understanding of who we are in God, the sound that we release should become all the more certain.

Gideon's men blew their trumpets in unison when the time was right. The sound that was released resonated in the darkness, and struck the Midianite camp with terror. It had been more than 150 years since sound brought down Jericho at the hands of Joshua and the Israelites. That was an impossible victory then, but the sounds of God and His people are a formidable force. When the heavenly Father has given divine directive, the best thing to do is obey. It may sound crazy and go against all logic, but it will produce victory every single time.

GUARANTEED
VICTORY

CHAPTER EIGHT
THE ART OF UNITY

There is a theme that is imperative for the body of Christ to understand. This theme is overarching throughout the account of Gideon's 300. It is oftentimes overlooked, but it's ultimately what empowered their victory over the insurmountable army of the Midianites. What was the greatest weapon that Gideon and his 300 possessed? Was their great weapon the jar, or the lamp, or maybe the trumpet? These were important, but they all fade away compared to the power of their *unity*. Were you expecting something else? Unity is one of the greatest things that God has ordained for us to flow in, but sadly, it escapes our understanding more than we know.

> Unity is one of the greatest things that God has ordained for us to flow in, but sadly, it escapes our understanding more than we know.

There is no doubt in my mind that Gideon and his 300 had to walk in unity in order to be useful in the hands of the King. They made the cut when it came to the separations of fear and power, but the unity required to defeat the Midianites was of greater value. Gideon gave his 300 directions that had to be followed to the exact detail. When they assembled in the mountains to begin waging war, they didn't have the luxury of an identity crisis or suggesting their own strategies. They came together in holy unity, and did exactly what God commanded of them to do.

> *Judges 7:19-20-*
> *So Gideon, and the hundred men that were with him, came unto*
> *the outside of the camp in the beginning of the middle watch; and*
> *they had but newly set the watch: and they blew the trumpets,*
> *and brake the pitchers that were in their hands. And the three*
> *companies blew the trumpets, and brake the pitchers, and held*
> *the lamps in their left hands, and the trumpets in their right*
> *hands to blow withal: and they cried, The sword of the Lord, and*
> *of Gideon. (KJV)*

What did the unity of Gideon's 300 look like? Can you imagine what it must have been like to behold? Each man took his place at exactly the right spot. They had to be in precise unity when they broke the jars covering their torches. The torches lit up the ridge line in perfect unison. Before the Midianites could properly panic at the sight of the corporate torches, they heard the deafening sound of 300 trumpets that we being blown with all the might of Gideon's men. After this initial blast of sound, there followed a sound, a decree of even greater terror. The mighty shout uttered into this scene of chaos was, "The sword of the Lord, and of Gideon!"

I am not exactly sure which element of this encounter frightened the Midianites more. It could have been seeing the light that pierced the darkness, or the sound of mighty men shouting in the night, but the results of Gideon's 300 cannot be argued. The Midiantes broke out into a feverish panic, and the host of the Midianites began to turn their swords on one another. Gideon's men continued to blast their trumpets, and stand their ground as they watched the slaughter continue. Fear was now fully evident in the camp of the Midianites, and it would destroy them utterly.

The Lord's Prayer

Unity is so imperative to the Lord, that it is one of the things that He personally prayed for. We have incorrectly assumed that we find the Lord's prayer in *Matthew 6*, but this is not actually the case. In *Matthew 6* we find Jesus instructing us how to pray, but we actually find His prayer later on in the book of *John*. The real "Lord's prayer" was the prayer of unity. Think about it, this was the personal prayer of Jesus right before He was turned over to His accusers so that He would be crucified. He could've been praying about many other things, but the unity of His people was paramount in His heart. His prayer of unity remains fresh today, and Jesus always gets what He prays for!

> *John 17:21-*
> *That they all may be one; as thou, Father, art in me, and I in thee, that they also may be one in us: that the world may believe that thou hast sent me. (KJV)*

There are themes of unity throughout the Scripture. There are many benefits that we can identify as a result of the unity of the brethren. When the body of Christ dwells together in unity, we find that which is good and pleasant. The truth is revealed in Psalms, that in the place of unity, God commands blessing! The Hebrew word for command is *mits'vah* and it means "commands of force or power as a General commands his troops." Wow! When the body of Christ walks in unity, they find themselves under the command of their heavenly General, and His command is the release of blessings with force and power.

> *Psalm 133:1-3-*
> *Behold, how good and how pleasant it is for brethren to dwell together in unity! It is like the precious ointment upon the head, that ran down upon the beard, even Aaron's beard: that went down to the skirts of his garments; As the dew of Hermon, and as*

*the dew that descended upon the mountains of Zion: for there the
Lord commanded the blessing, even life for evermore. (KJV)*

It is time for the Church to lay down its denominational differences
and hang ups! The world has never witnessed such a disjointed and
broken family unit. We all desire blessing, but we neglect the place
of commanded blessing. We all want to honor the Lord, but we
neglect His earnest prayer of unity. It is time for us to unify within
our own cities and counties. Can you imagine what a unified body of
believers could accomplish in one town?! The Holy Spirit has
already anointed us for unity, our end of stewardship is to keep
unity.

Keeping Unity

I sincerely believe that unity is an anointing. When I observe the
tendencies of humanity for total independence, it is no surprise that
so many are suspect of attempts by others to create unity. I have seen
such attempts put on by church after church for years. You have seen
many of these attempts yourself. How many times have you heard of
a pastor's prayer breakfast, regional church prayer initiatives, or
unity summits? I am not knocking any of these ideas, but personally,
I have never seen any lasting fruit from such functions. Why?
Because in our attempts to "create" unity, we usually overlook that
we are anointed to "keep" unity.

> In our attempts to "create" unity, we usually overlook that
> we are anointed to "keep" unity.

Unity is birthed in the presence of God. Where God is, unity thrives.
When I think of the many great moves of God over the last two
centuries, they all had at least one thing in common. They each had
the presence of the Lord. Unity doesn't sacrifice diversity, but unity
empowers it. God never envisioned a "cookie cutter" family of
believers that are not unique or individual. When we understand that
God loves and values our diversity, we will find just how anointed
we are to keep the unity He has ordained us to walk in.

I once heard a well respected man of God challenge the lack of diversity he saw in many local churches. His heart was so fixed on the beauty of the multifaceted family of God, that he warned people of their involvement in a ministry that lacked diversity. He went so far as to challenge if such ministries were actually valid or not in the Kingdom! I know that sounds drastic, but I tend to agree with the heart of what he believed. No one has been able to convince me yet that God intended for there to be "black" churches, "white" churches, "baptist" churches, "pentecostal" churches, or any of the various expressions we tend to use to separate ourselves from others in the vast body of Christ. We are called to be THE CHURCH! Let's keep the unity!

> *Ephesians 4:2-6-*
> *With all lowliness and meekness, with longsuffering, forbearing one another in love; Endeavoring to keep the unity of the Spirit in the bond of peace. There is one body, and one Spirit, even as ye are called in one hope of your calling; One Lord, one faith, one baptism, One God and Father of all, who is above all, and through all, and in you all.* (KJV)

The two greatest forces that strengthen corporate unity, are peace and love. Again, this never means that there are no disagreements or conflicts. When we esteem our brothers and sisters in God with peace and love, we will commit to keeping unity, especially when we have differences. When I truly love you, I will stay in unity with you! I am a part of some pretty intense discussion groups on Facebook, and there are times when I have to remind myself, these are my brothers and sisters. Sometimes being right is less important than keeping unity. After all, I'm willing to submit whatever is important to me, to what is resonating in the heart of God.

> *Colossians 3:12-14-*
> *Therefore, as God's chosen people, holy and dearly loved, clothe yourselves with compassion, kindness, humility, gentleness and patience. Bear with each other and forgive one another if any of you has a grievance against someone. Forgive as the Lord forgave you. And over all these virtues put on love, which binds them all together in perfect unity. (NIV)*

True peace and love flow out of proper identity. When we see ourselves as the righteous family of God, it takes unity to a whole new level. Our righteous identity allows us to walk in forgiveness, compassion, and gentleness. This produces the effortless ability to keep unity. As the corporate identity of the Church matures, we will walk in the greatest love that the world has ever witnessed. This love will bind us together. It will not simply bind us together in unity, but it will bind us together in "perfect unity". This is what it looks like when the prayer of Jesus is answered.

> Our righteous identity allows us to walk in forgiveness, compassion, and gentleness.

Gideon's men knew something of unity. There had to be a core of identity that was substantial in each one of these men. They trusted God, Gideon, and each other. We have no record of who these men were individually, because they have only ever been identified as a corporate unit. They were Gideon's 300. Their desire for unity took them beyond their need for personal praise and recognition. Their desire to be used by God wasn't muddied by their need to make a name for themselves. Somehow, they were satisfied that God would get the glory, and that is what mattered most to them. I believe the Church globally, is on the verge of knowing something about unity, and when it does, the world will be rocked to its foundations!

GUARANTEED
VICTORY

CHAPTER NINE
COME OUT OF HIDING

When we look at the account of Gideon, we typically stop once the 300 have blown their trumpets and the Midianites panic and run, but this is not the end of the story. What follows the trumpet blast and the illumination of torches, is something we see time and again in Scripture. Once the victory is witnessed by a few, everyone else tends to join in to be a part of it. In the case of Gideon, less than one percent of his company was qualified to be used by the Lord, but once the victory was witnessed, the men of Israel showed up in droves to pursue those who remained of the Midianites.

This is when you truly have to walk in peace and love with your heavenly family. This would be the prime opportunity to condescend and ridicule those who didn't have the courage or guts to stand up during the hard times, but this was not the heart of Gideon. You see, it was Gideon who made the call for the men of Israel to join in the fight! He had the wisdom to keep the conflict off of Israel and on the Midianites. It was because of this heart attitude, that all of Israel was able to come out of hiding, and share in the victory that God had gained with the hands of Gideon and his 300.

> *Judges 7:22-25-*
> *And the three hundred blew the trumpets, and the Lord set every man's sword against his fellow, even throughout all the host: and the host fled to Bethshittah in Zererath, and to the border of Abelmeholah, unto Tabbath. And the men of Israel gathered themselves together out of Naphtali, and out of Asher, and out of all Manasseh, and pursued after the Midianites. And Gideon sent messengers throughout all mount Ephraim, saying, come down against the Midianites, and take before them the waters unto Bethbarah and Jordan. Then all the men of Ephraim gathered themselves together, and took the waters unto Bethbarah and Jordan. And they took two princes of the Midianites, Oreb and Zeeb; and they slew Oreb upon the rock Oreb, and Zeeb they slew at the winepress of Zeeb, and pursued Midian, and brought the heads of Oreb and Zeeb to Gideon on the other side Jordan.*
> *(KJV)*

Once the enemy was on the run, the heart of Gideon remained true to the cause. He didn't mock the fearful of Israel. Instead, he invited them to join in the victory. Before you knew it, men from Naphtali, Asher, Manasseh, and Ephraim gave chase to the fleeing Midianites! The once fearful men of Israel, suddenly became warriors. A remnant led the way for a massive campaign to eradicate the host that had defied God and His people. We have no idea how much the men of Gideon grew that day, but we can tell from Scripture, that they grew by many.

Cut Off The Head!

The masses tend to gain courage when someone crosses the line of opposition. This is not a new occurrence. It has happened all throughout history, and there are multiple accounts we can identify in Scripture. To find the most famous encounter of the fearful joining the courageous, I have to go back to the encounter of David and Goliath again. In the midst of the entire army of Israel, there wasn't even one who would stand up against Goliath. Once David came on the scene, he was anointed to cross the threshold of opposition. Once David confronted Goliath and defeated him, the fearful Israelites gained immediate courage!

> *1 Samuel 17:50-51-*
> *So David prevailed over the Philistine with a sling and with a stone, and smote the Philistine, and slew him; but there was no sword in the hand of David. Therefore David ran, and stood upon the Philistine, and took his sword, and drew it out of the sheath thereof, and slew him, and cut off his head therewith. And when the Philistines saw their champion was dead, they fled. (KJV)*

The key to conquering opposition is to cut off its head! The strength of the Philistines was not found in their mass of soldiers, it was contained in their figure head. The Midianites counted their strength in numbers, but their numbers counted for nothing when fear was in the camp. I have found that the understanding of this principle has been a valuable tool for my life. I must keep my trust in the Lord, and take my focus off of the distractions that tend to bog me down. I am then able to see the source, root, or head of the problem, and I can then deal with the issue effectively. If David had focused on the whole Philistine army, he wouldn't have been victorious. David knew what he was anointed for, and he overcame Goliath flawlessly.

I heard one minister teach that when David cut off the head of Goliath, he then had every right to turn the sword on Israel. Thankfully, David understood that his conflict was not with Israel, but with the Philistines. He and Gideon had the same heart once they had served as the spearhead in the plan of God. David had nothing in his heart against Israel, but instead, it was his joy to watch the army of Israel pursue those who had once kept them paralyzed in fear. David went for the head, and watched the people rise to the occasion. When God has anointed you for a specific task, don't turn on the people!

1 Samuel 17:52-53-
And the men of Israel and of Judah arose, and shouted, and
pursued the Philistines, until thou come to the valley, and to
the gates of Ekron. And the wounded of the Philistines fell
down by the way to Shaaraim, even unto Gath, and unto
Ekron. And the children of Israel returned from chasing after
the Philistines, and they spoiled their tents. (KJV)

Jesus Is Our Champion

The earliest prophetic utterance we find concerning Jesus, has to do
with His total victory. He crossed the ultimate threshold of
opposition, and is overjoyed for us to walk in His accomplished
work! This is much of the reason why I get so frustrated with the
unending warfare and fatigue that so many in the body of Christ buy
into. I have been of that mindset before, and remained exhausted,
frustrated, and paranoid. When I began to focus on the supreme
victory and strength of the Lord, I found that my reasons to war
became more and more slim. Jesus crushed the head of our
opposition once and for all! He was completely successful in His
conquest!

Genesis 3:15-
And I will put enmity between you and the woman, and between
your offspring and hers; he will crush your head, and you will
strike his heel. (ESV)

The prophetic word concerning the victory of Jesus that was uttered
in Genesis, was fulfilled in the gospels. Jesus put an end to the
influence of the adversary, as well as the demands of the law. I
believe more and more, that the greatest adversary humanity has
ever known, was the old covenant law. The word promised that the
heel of the seed would be bruised, and it was. It also promised that
the head of the serpent would be crushed, and it was. Our heavenly
'David' cut the head off of any 'Goliath' that we would ever face!
He is calling for us to come out of hiding and witness and believe
what He has already done.

Jesus put an end to the influence of the adversary, as well as the demands of the law.

The amphitheater of the conquest of Jesus, was on the hill called Golgotha. As Jesus hung upon the cross, with His arms stretched between two covenants, He dealt the deathblow to the consequences of sin. It was from this place of supreme authority that Jesus gave His life freely. In the giving of Himself, He brought a reconnection between mankind and God that had not been enjoyed since the nation of Israel was wandering in the wilderness. He birthed a brand new nation out of the loins of His spirit, as was evidenced by the flow of blood and water that poured from His heart. A brand new covenant was birthed in that day, and we have been the beneficiaries of it ever since. When you recognize Jesus as the supreme Victor, you will find it hard to identify with the "poor old Jesus" mentality ever again.

Today, I see a breed of believers emerging who are confident in the Lord. They may appear to be a remnant today, but looks can be deceiving. It will only take a few people who actually take Jesus at His word, for the floodgates of the nations to open. When we see that our Captain has already secured our victory, we will embrace our identity as those who are called to impact the nations with the love and freedom of God that they so desperately crave. I have never bought into the thought of a weak, spineless Church, but I have seen it do an awful lot of sleeping. There are voices today that are causing the Church to stir to action, and to become reacquainted with the extravagant goodness of their Beloved!

Romans 8:2-4-
For the law of the Spirit of life has set you free in Christ Jesus from the law of sin and death. For God has done what the law, weakened by the flesh, could not do. By sending his own Son in the likeness of sinful flesh and for sin, he condemned sin in the flesh, in order that the righteous requirement of the law might be fulfilled in us, who walk not according to the flesh but according to the Spirit. (ESV)

GUARANTEED
VICTORY

CHAPTER TEN
LIVING IN GUARANTEED VICTORY

Are we tired of living beneath our potential yet? We are called to live a life that many of us have never dreamed possible. We have settled for a bar of success in Christ that has been set very low, but the time of radical change is upon us. The sum total of our hopes and dreams are found in Jesus, and they have never been found in anything else. Somewhere along the way, we have so complicated what our lives are supposed to be, that we have complicated them out of being effective. The Lord is calling us to rise above the chatter and to see from a renewed perspective. We must stop living the lives we have constructed through our own efforts and struggles, and yield to the life of Christ that is resident on the inside.

Galatians 2:20-
I have been crucified with Christ. It is no longer I who live, but
Christ who lives in me. And the life I now live in the flesh I live
by faith in the Son of God, who loved me and gave himself for
me. (ESV)

This may sound way too simple, but it is time for us to return to
faith. As beneficiaries of the new covenant, our faith is designed to
thrive and be fruitful. What is the fruit of our faith? The fruit our
faith is the public unveiling of Jesus in our lives, families, careers,
and ministries. Jesus had to bring an end to the old covenant so that
we could be restored back to faith. Abraham, not Moses, is our
father of faith! The new covenant in Christ is more beautiful than
any of us really understand. It was through this extravagant display
of love, that God made us His habitation forever.

You could say that the underlying theme of this book has been to
help us grow in faith. How can we not grow in faith when we see all
that Lord has done for us? Jesus freed us from fear, helped us
conquer insurmountable odds, delivered unto us our holy identity,
defeated our adversary, and made us truly alive for the first time! It's
difficult to maintain an attitude of defeat and depression when we
continually see Jesus in these ways. We must commit in faith, to
show the nations of the earth the real Lord, and not the one fashioned
by the systems of religion. I firmly believe that how we see Jesus in
our own lives, will impact how others will see Him.

The Great Secret Of Gideon

The great secret of Gideon, is that there is no secret. He was a man
that was full of doubt and fear, just like most of us. He struggled
with his identity, and he certainly never had himself pegged as a
national war hero. At face value, he was an abject failure when it
came to building an army. Less than one percent of his group
remained, once the fearful and the foolish were sifted. By today's
standards, Gideon would be laughed out of the who's who of the
church club, and would probably never be heard from again.
Fortunately, the Lord is still searching for men and women like
Gideon. He is looking for those, who despite their fear and

insecurities, are willing to take a step of faith in the face of ridiculous odds.

When Gideon saw that God was with Him, something in his heart shifted. The vital powers and strength of God came upon him, and breathed into him new purpose. I have seen this very thing happen to people all over the world. When they are exposed to the goodness and grace of God, they are suddenly equipped with vital power and strength. When you believe that God is mad at you and is inconvenienced by you, it is hard to view Him or your purpose with much optimism. I am thankful that today there are more and more men and women who are representing God well, and as a result, people are falling in love all over again with a God they thought they knew.

Based on what we read in Scripture, we can assume that Gideon didn't know much personally about the Lord. We would label Gideon as a babe or newcomer to the things of God. Even though he didn't technically know the Lord very well, we have proof that he already loved Him. This is evidenced by his desire to worship the Lord without being told to do so, once he heard the dreams of his enemies. God is calling for all of us to return to our first love in Him. He is freeing us from the issues in our lives that have caused us to become hardened and jaded towards Him. It doesn't matter if your relationship with the Lord is a day old or fifty years old, He wants to compel you afresh with His extravagant love.

Where Do We Go From Here?

How would you live life if you knew you couldn't fail? How would your life change if you truly believed that God was for you? I want to challenge you to no longer think of these possibilities as unattainable, they are meant to be a part of your life now! If you feel like Gideon, and are facing impossible odds, I want you to know that God has already prepared your path of victory. He has already qualified you as a person of great quality, and has given you the tools necessary to have victory over fear and condemnation. You are of the quality of Gideon's 300, and the Father has invited you to witness His supreme victory concerning all of the things you could ever encounter.

God is inviting us to see from a different perspective. When we see what God sees, we will always be looking at *Someone*. Jesus longs to be seen by us. Everything that we can possibly need in life is directly connected to a greater revelation of Jesus. He brings clarity and focus to the areas of our lives that are lacking. As the magnificence of Jesus is revealed, the poor prosper, the weak are made strong, and the sick are healed from all manner of disease. Jesus is presently preaching the good news to the world. All those who hear Him, and see, will walk in the life of abundance!

> *1 John 3:2-*
> *Beloved, we are God's children now, and what we will be has not yet appeared; but we know that when he appears we shall be like him, because we shall see him as he is. (ESV)*

This verse shows us just how imperative it is for us to see the Lord. It is so important in fact, that we are told that when we *see* Him, we will be *like* Him. The Greek word for see in 1 John 3:2 is *horao* and it means "to stare." The Lord is not asking us to casually look at Him, but He wants us to see Him with our eyes fixed intently upon Him. He wants us to see Him in the Scriptures. He wants us to see Him in our worship, our work, our fun and our family. He is destined to be our all consuming desire, as it is from this perspective that life begins to make sense.

Today I am asking the Lord to set your heart ablaze. He will do this by revealing Himself in amazing ways to you. When you open your Bible, He will be there. When you talk to your spouse, you will feel His heart. When you pray, you will hear His voice. The Lord is systematically freeing us from ignorance, and He is challenging us to believe the truths of Who He is. These were the same issues that the two men on the road to Emmaus dealt with, but when Jesus revealed Himself to them, they walked away with their hearts burning afresh. Listen, look, love and respond to the goodness of the Lord, and your heart will burn with an intensity that you have never known before.

You are a vessel of clay that has been crafted by the hands of the Almighty. He has put within you the greatest light that the world can ever know. He has given you a voice that blasts like a trumpet into the static and the chaos of darkness. He has already prepared your path, and lights each step, that you might place all of your hope in Him. He didn't bring you this far, to expect you to figure out the rest on your own. Put your head to His heart and hear your name resonate within its beats. Do you see what I see? I see your path of *Guaranteed Victory* already prepared.

GUARANTEED
VICTORY

CHAPTER ELEVEN
THE PEACE THAT FOLLOWS

Gideon and his 300 were used mightily in the victory against the Midianites. After the main event, Gideon, his men, and the tribes of Israel pursued the remnants of their enemies until they were all subdued. As we read through Judges 8 we see a glimpse into the rest of the life of Gideon. Once the war was over, he had lots of kids and lived to a good old age. Because of his faithfulness, we find that Israel was in peace and quiet for a generation. Gideon didn't just personally enjoy the peace that came from his obedience, but the whole nation enjoyed it as well.

What was Gideon's greatest testimony? Was his greatest testimony the amazing, unlikely, impossible victory over the Midianite army or was it the peace that lasted Israel for a generation? Gideon had a reputation that stayed with him for the remainder of his life. Perhaps some guys would get around a campfire and recall the conquest accomplished by the hand of God. Men always assign glory to the grand event, but they rarely discern the lasting glory of the fruit that remains. Gideon was not simply a "one time" warrior, but he was a godly man and a good father.

What Is Peace?

Mankind is always in the pursuit of peace. Everyone wants to be free of war, hostilities, quarrels and disagreements, but the only true peace that can be found is in Jesus. Peace is more than a state of being, peace is a Person. Peace is so important to the attributes of the Lord that He is called the *Prince of Peace* in Isaiah 9:6. This name of the Lord is directly connected to His earthly ministry and the work He finished through His death, burial, resurrection and ascension. Jesus destroyed the works of the adversary, restored humanity and established a Kingdom without end. In other words, the greatest campaign of peace that the world has ever known was accomplished through the person of Jesus.

> *Isaiah 9:6-*
> *For to us a child is born, to us a son is given; and the*
> *government shall be upon his shoulder, and his name shall be*
> *called Wonderful Counselor, Mighty God, Everlasting Father,*
> *Prince of Peace. (ESV)*

There is also the promise of peace that passes our understanding. This peace keeps our hearts and minds focused on the goodness of God and steers us away from all of the worries, distraction and chatter of life. There is no understanding required to walk in the peace of God. Even in the midst of what appears to be total chaos, the peace of God is there to comfort us and to remind us of who we are. We are not designed to be victims of circumstance. We are designed to be victors through circumstance. Peace is a vital component to living the life of Guaranteed Victory. Embrace He Who is peace today, and it will only enrich your life for the better.

Peace In The Storm

One of my favorite displays of what it looks like to walk in supernatural peace, is found in the earthly ministry of Jesus. We should all remember the account of when Jesus had His disciples get into a boat and told them to sail to the other side of the lake. This story is part of Sunday school curriculum 101. As amazing as this account is, there is a subtle truth that we can miss when it comes to how peace is revealed in the life of the believer. When we go back and examine this famous account, we will find that the call for peace was not so much in Jesus' ability to supernaturally calm the storm, but it was in the power of His word.

> *Luke 8:22-25-*
> *One day he got into a boat with his disciples, and he said to them, "Let us go across to the other side of the lake." So they set out, and as they sailed he fell asleep. And a windstorm came down on the lake, and they were filling with water and were in danger. And they went and woke him, saying, "Master, Master, we are perishing!" And he awoke and rebuked the wind and the raging waves, and they ceased, and there was a calm. He said to them, "Where is your faith?" And they were afraid, and they marveled, saying to one another, "Who then is this, that he commands even winds and water, and they obey him?"*

The disciples were amazed when they witnessed Jesus calm the winds and the water. It would have been better if they had simply remembered the words He spoke before they departed. Jesus had spoken a guarantee into the midst of their journey. Jesus' words were, "Let us go across to the other side of the lake". These words are full of peace that passes understanding. As soon as the storm began, the disciples should have encouraged one another with the word of the Lord! When He says that you're going to go to other side of the lake, you are going to go to the other side of the lake. It is the substantial word of God that allows you to maintain peace in the midst of the greatest of storms.

*It is the substantial word of God that allows you to maintain peace
in the midst of the greatest of storms.*

Do you have a word from the Lord that has carried you through a great storm? Many have received a word about the restoration of their families that has given them peace during very hard times. Perhaps a word about promotion has kept you working faithfully at a job you would've left long ago. The words of the living God are not just meant to be cataloged in a diary somewhere to admire from time to time. The words of God are full of life! They can change the outcome of conflict and the course of nations. What has God said to you? Plant yourself firmly in what He has spoken in your heart and live the life of peace that doesn't need to be understood.

Agents Of Peace

Once we grasp personal peace, we are then ready to share peace with others. The best way to share peace with the world is by demonstrating the goodness of God to them. The peace of God is heard when we share the gospel of the Kingdom of God. It is experienced when we show humanity the benefits of the New Covenant. It is solidified when we show them the love of God that passes their wildest dreams or imaginations. We are agents of peace, who are called to bring treaties of peace to the nations of the earth. The sons and daughters of God are equipped with peace. Where there is peace, there is no fear. We can walk into places ruled by fear, confusion and chaos, and release peace that brings an end to it all.

John 14:27-
Peace I leave with you; my peace I give to you. Not as the world gives do I give to you. Let not your hearts be troubled, neither let them be afraid. (ESV)

My dad has been a great father to me, both naturally and spiritually. I remember countless times growing up when people would come to him for counsel. They would walk into his office full of frustration and anger, and many times were already surrendered to their circumstances in defeat. My dad would then begin to release this peace and calm into the scenario that was tangible. Often times, it was peace that brought the clarity to know what to do. I would see an angry couple leave his office with tears of joy. I saw many people down and distraught walk away with renewed hope and wise counsel. I wanted this kind of peace in my life too.

What I found in my pursuit of peace, was the undeniable connection between peace and healthy identity in Christ. When you don't know who you are, it is impossible to walk in meaningful peace. My dad wasn't simply activating the gift of peace, he was living out of the fruit of peace. Where was that fruit cultivated? It was cultivated through times of personal worship, prayer and relationship with God. In other words, as his identity in God grew, his peace became all the more obvious. When people came to get counsel from my dad, they were coming to be ministered to by a peacemaker.

Gideon was also a peacemaker. He may not have known it at the time, but his actions would cause the nation of Israel to be at peace for a generation. What simple keys empowered Gideon to be used so mightily by the hand of God? Simple trust and obedience is what caused Gideon to be an unlikely peacemaker. Perhaps most of us feel that we aren't even close to being qualified as peacemakers, but peace is directly connected to our identity as the family of God. He is looking for someone who will take Him at His word and trust in what He has already established.

> *Matthew 5:9-*
> *"Blessed are the peacemakers, for they shall be called sons of God." (ESV)*

Take A Breath

The voice of the heavenly Father is calling your name. He is ready for you to live life the way that He has always desired; a life free from fear, doubt, shame and despair. He is clearing your vision to see Him as He truly is. He has always been for you. He has given you vital powers and strength, and like Gideon, He is calling forth the purity of your identity afresh. You are His beloved. You are His son. You are His hands and feet in the earth, and it is with the greatest of joy and excitement that He calls you His own. Do you hear the sound of His voice?

He is calling you beyond your seemingly insurmountable odds. He is showing you the power of your life and light in the midst of hostility and chaos. You are *a victor*, because He is *the Victor*! Don't allow the past to cast doubt on your present and future. God has erased your past. He has empowered your present. He has secured your future. He fashioned you meticulously, equipped you sufficiently, and He has empowered you substantially. The earth is looking for you to emerge. It is waiting on hinged anticipation to see what you are all about. Lift up your head. Open your eyes. Take a deep breath. You were born for this. You were born to live in Guaranteed Victory!

> God has erased your past. He has empowered your present. He has secured your future.

GUARANTEED
VICTORY

BONUS SECTION
HAVE YOU CONSIDERED THIS?

If you're good at something, don't do it for free.

In 1 Samuel 17 we find the famous account of David slaying Goliath. Before David slew Goliath, He enquired what the reward would be. David understood that if you're good at something, don't do it for free. There is no mention of David killing a man before he faced Goliath, but we do know for certain that he had killed a bear and a lion (1 Sam. 17:34-36). David was good at killing large, dangerous beasts. I don't know about you, but I would much rather face a large man, than be at the mercy of a lion or bear!

I consider myself a brave man, but if I saw a bear or a lion come to the edge of my father's field, my father would've lost a sheep that day. This was not the stuff that David was made of. He ran to the bear and the lion so that he could save one sheep! David's brothers didn't understand this quality about their little brother. David did not come to SEE the battle against the Philistines, but he came to BE IN the battle. When David responded to the cause of the nation of Israel we receive a powerful glimpse of what this "secretly anointed" king was made of.

God and math

One of the themes of this book is that God looks more at quality than He does quantity. In other words, God understands that being effective is not often associated with a large mass of people. God doesn't count people, but He weighs them. The account of Gideon gives us direct insight into this truth. 32,000 men was too large of a group for God to use, but 300 men was just the right amount. The large gathering of 32,000 weighed less than the 300 that God ultimately used in the victory against the Midiantes.

> Matthew 18:20-
> For where **two or** three are gathered together in my name,
> there am I in the midst of them. (KJV) (Emphasis Mine)

We could build an air tight case for the mega church if the promise of God's presence would come where 2,000 or more are gathered. Instead, we are told that where two or more are gathered together, He is in the midst of them. It doesn't matter how big or how small your local church is, just be sure of your own weight in the spirit.

The God of the overkill

> Deuteronomy 32:30-
> How could one have chased a thousand, and two have put ten
> thousand to flight, unless their Rock had sold them, and the
> Lord had given them up? (ESV)

Deuteronomy 32:30 shows us the principle that 1 can put a 1,000 to flight and 2 can put 10,000 to flight. This verse was written concerning the enemies of Israel overtaking them, but this math also works for the believer, as long as you are following the orders of the Lord and you find yourself in the right place at the right time. When

the Rock is for you, who can be against you? Using this theory (technically), 10 of Gideon's men could have put a trillion men to flight. The Midianites never had a chance. If they could have gotten every man on earth to gather against Gideon and his 300, they would still have failed miserably! When God invites you to a battle, it is so you can witness the victory!

Warriors without swords

Can you imagine the amount of trust that Gideon's 300 had? We never read any accounts in Scripture that say that his 300 had anything other than full confidence in what Gideon was hearing from the Lord. I would think that if there were any moment to doubt what Gideon was doing, it would have been when there were no swords handed out for the battle against the Midianites. The weapons they were given were a clay pot, a torch and a trumpet. There's no doubt that these men were of a great quality! They followed orders, no questions asked, and will be remembered throughout history as a result.

Don't hide your light under works

The torches that were kept under the jars by Gideon's men were not hidden, but rather temporarily concealed. Once the jars were broken, the light pierced the darkness. We must guard against the tendency to keep our light, Who is Christ, hidden from the world. How do we keep our light hidden? The way most of us conceal our light is by covering it with works. I had a friend recently share this truth with me and I thought it was excellent!

> *Matthew 5:15-*
> *Nor do people light a lamp and put it under a basket, but on*
> *a stand, and it gives light to all in the house. (ESV)*

In the above verse we are exhorted to not put our lamp under a basket. The basket that is being referred to in this verse is a bushel basket. A bushel basket was a basket used in the fields to bring in the harvest. In other words, a bushel basket was a *work* basket. The easiest way for us to cover the light that is inside us, is by piling up heaps of works on top of it. The Father wants to free us from the works of our own strength, so that the light of God can burn brightly in and through us.

HESTER MINISTRIES

CHECK OUT OUR WEBSITE FOR:

BOOKS
TEACHINGS
VIDEOS
And LOTS OF GREAT RESOURCES

www.HESTERMINISTRIES.org

BECOMING GLORIOUS

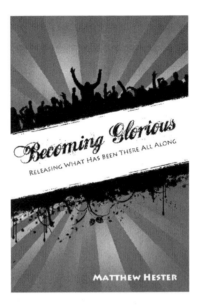

Are you ready to be all that God has called you to be? Are you ready to walk in the fullness of your destiny and purpose? Everything you need from the Father has already been given to you. Now is the time to respond to the glorious God Who lives on the inside of you!

THE TREE OF LIFE

Jesus is the Tree of Life. He has been planted deep inside our hearts and we are called to tend to the fruit of His righteousness. When we have a revelation of the depth of the roots of the Lord, we then live out of a stability that is unshakeable.

BORN TO BE KINGS

We are born as the royalty of God. Our journey in the Kingdom is the greatest journey known to mankind. We were the first thought in the mind of God, and His plan has always been that of a family. Take the journey to Kingship and find out who you really are.

Made in the USA
Columbia, SC
27 August 2021